How to Use

History Pockets

*H*istory Pockets—*Life in Plymouth Colony* presents young students with a vivid picture of everyday life in this famous American settlement. The engaging activities are stored in labeled pockets and bound into a decorative cover. Students will be proud to see their accumulated projects presented all together. At the end of the book, evaluation sheets have been added for teacher use.

Make a Pocket

1. Use a 12" x 18" (30.5 x 45.5 cm) piece of construction paper for each pocket. Fold up 6" (15 cm) to make a 12" (30.5 cm) square.

2. Staple the right side of each pocket closed.

3. Punch two or three holes in the left side of each pocket.

Assemble the Pocket Book

1. Reproduce the cover illustration on page 3 for each student.

2. Direct students to color and cut out the illustration and glue it onto a 12" (30.5 cm) square of construction paper to make the cover.

3. Punch two or three holes in the left side of the cover.

4. Fasten the cover and the pockets together. You might use string, ribbon, twine, raffia, or binder rings.

Every Pocket Has...

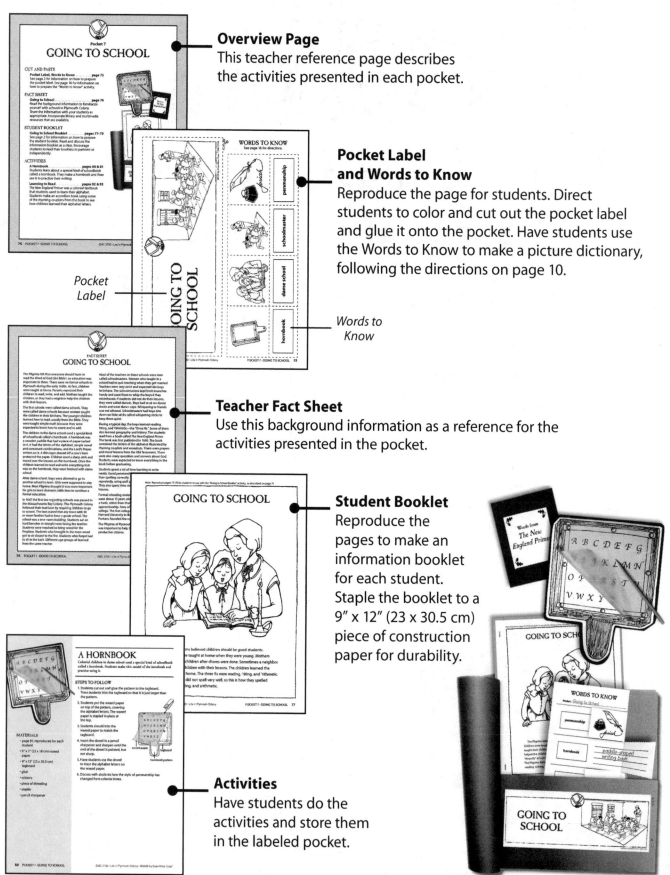

Overview Page
This teacher reference page describes the activities presented in each pocket.

Pocket Label

Pocket Label and Words to Know
Reproduce the page for students. Direct students to color and cut out the pocket label and glue it onto the pocket. Have students use the Words to Know to make a picture dictionary, following the directions on page 10.

Words to Know

Teacher Fact Sheet
Use this background information as a reference for the activities presented in the pocket.

Student Booklet
Reproduce the pages to make an information booklet for each student. Staple the booklet to a 9" x 12" (23 x 30.5 cm) piece of construction paper for durability.

Activities
Have students do the activities and store them in the labeled pocket.

EMC 3700 • Life in Plymouth Colony • ©2003 by Evan-Moor Corp.

Note: Reproduce this cover for students to color, cut out, and glue to the cover of their Life in Plymouth Colony book.

LIFE IN PLYMOUTH COLONY

Name:

VOYAGE TO THE NEW WORLD

CUT AND PASTE

Pocket Label, Words to Know .... **page 5**
See page 2 for information on how to prepare
the pocket label. See page 16 for information on
how to prepare the "Words to Know" activity.

FACT SHEET

Voyage to the New World................. **page 6**
Read the background information to familiarize
yourself with the voyage to the New World.
Share the information with your students as
appropriate. Incorporate library and multimedia
resources that are available.

STUDENT BOOKLET

**Voyage to the
New World Booklet** .... **pages 7–9**
See page 2 for information on how to prepare
the student booklet. Read and discuss the
information booklet as a class. Encourage
students to read their booklets to partners or
independently.

ACTIVITIES

The Pilgrims' Journey.. **pages 10 & 11**
The Pilgrims made the journey from Europe to the New World crossing the Atlantic Ocean.
Students learn the sequence of events of the journey and glue them onto the map on
page 11.

***Mayflower* Model** .... **pages 12–14**
Students learn about the great ship that brought the Pilgrims over to the New World when
they make a model of the *Mayflower*.

Packing for the Voyage .... **page 15**
Students pretend they are traveling with the Pilgrims. They cut out the trunk pattern and
glue it to white construction paper, cutting around it to make a border. Students fold the
trunk. Then they draw and write four precious items they would take with them on the
inside of the trunk and decorate it.

Words to Know .... **pages 16–18**
In this pocket, students begin a "Words to Know" picture dictionary using the words
presented on the pocket label page. A pocket label page with Words to Know is included
in each pocket.

    EMC 3700 · Life in Plymouth Colony · ©2003 by Evan-Moor Corp.

hardtack

voyage

New World

Pilgrim

VOYAGE TO THE NEW WORLD

VOYAGE TO THE NEW WORLD

The Pilgrims' decision to make a home in the New World was a difficult and expensive one. They hired two ships to take them across the Atlantic Ocean. The *Mayflower* was to carry most of the passengers, and a smaller ship, the *Speedwell,* was to accompany the *Mayflower*. The Pilgrims planned to use the *Speedwell* as a fishing boat in the New World.

The Pilgrims left England on September 6, 1620, on the two ships. The *Speedwell* and the *Mayflower* carried 120 passengers and were forced back twice by dangerous leaks in the *Speedwell*. At the English port of Plymouth, some of the *Speedwell's* passengers joined the *Mayflower,* and on September 16, the historic voyage across the Atlantic Ocean began.

This time the *Mayflower* carried 102 passengers and a crew of about 30. The number of Pilgrims on board was 35. The other 67 passengers were hired men, paid servants, and "strangers" the Pilgrims brought along. The term *strangers* meant people who wanted to make a life in the New World, but who did not belong to the separatist group of Pilgrims.

Master Christopher Jones, the skipper of the ship, was worried about sailing the Atlantic because winter was approaching and the seas would be stormy. The Pilgrims insisted on leaving, and the ship set out. The *Mayflower* was a merchant ship, not a passenger ship. The ship was about 90 feet (27 m) long and 26 feet (8 m) wide. It weighed about 180 tons (162 metric tonnes). It was built to carry wine and other cargo.

Life aboard the *Mayflower* was difficult. There was no privacy and finding a place to sleep was hard. The passengers had to live in a space between the decks. Some of the passengers slept on wooden pallets attached to the walls, while others slept on hammocks and on the floor. A few people even slept in the shallop, which was a small boat that was stowed on the gun deck.

Because the ship was so crowded, sanitary conditions were terrible. The people bathed while the limited fresh water supply lasted. They had to use chamber pots for toilets. Cockroaches, flies, and gray rats shared the same spaces with the passengers. During the stormy weather, the people had to stay below deck where it was dark and wet, and many people got seasick.

The passengers and crew ate meat and vegetables at the beginning of the trip. Later on, when the fresh food was gone, the people ate hard biscuits called hardtack, dried meat, and dried fish. They drank ale or water. Because the journey was so long, food supplies were very low by the time the ship anchored.

To keep their spirits up, passengers prayed, sang, and told stories to the 32 children on the ship. A child, Oceanus Hopkins, was born on the voyage, and another, Peregrine White, was born when the *Mayflower* landed. There were two dogs aboard to entertain the passengers. During the 66-day voyage, only one person, William Burton, died.

After nearly two months at sea, the ship was blown off course by a strong ocean storm. The ship headed for Cape Cod in Massachusetts instead of the intended destination of the Virginia Colony. Before landing, the Pilgrims wrote the Mayflower Compact. The compact was an agreement signed by all the men on board, and it stated that they would choose their own leaders and make their own laws once they arrived at the new colony. The women were not allowed to participate in this agreement.

The *Mayflower* landed on November 11, 1620, in a safe harbor at the tip of Cape Cod. There is no proof that the Pilgrims actually stepped off the ship onto a special rock that is referred to as Plymouth Rock. It is said that Plymouth Rock can be called a symbolic steppingstone from the Old World to the New World.

VOYAGE TO THE
NEW WORLD

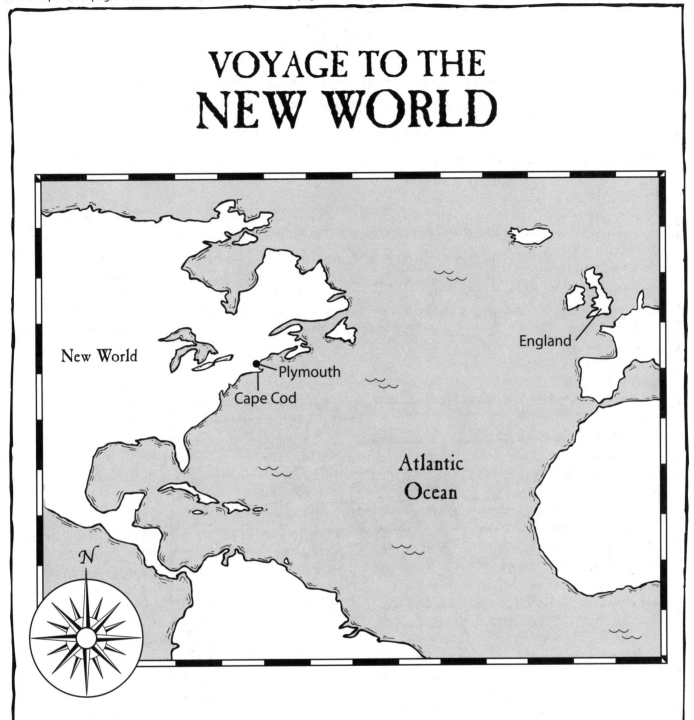

On September 6, 1620, a group of **Pilgrims** left England on a ship called the *Mayflower*. They were going to sail across the Atlantic Ocean to the **New World**. They wanted to start a new life. The *Mayflower* was a sailing ship. It was 90 feet (27 m) long and 26 feet (8 m) wide. It weighed 180 tons (162 metric tonnes). The Pilgrims were sure the *Mayflower* would get them to the New World safely.

There were 102 passengers on the *Mayflower*. There were 30 crew members to help on the ship. The captain's name was Christopher Jones. He worried that the ship was going to be too crowded. His ship had not been built to carry people. It was built to carry barrels of supplies.

Life on the *Mayflower* was hard. The passengers lived in a space between the decks. It was cold and wet. They had to sleep on the floor or in hammocks. There were no bathrooms or showers. They used containers called chamber pots for bathrooms. During stormy weather the people got seasick.

In the beginning, people ate fresh meat and vegetables. They had ale and water to drink. After the fresh food was gone, people ate dried meat and dried fish. They also had dried fruit and cheese. The food supplies got very low at the end of the trip. They ate hard biscuits called **hardtack**. There were cockroaches, flies, and rats that tried to eat the food.

The Pilgrims tried to keep their spirits up on the **voyage**. They spent time praying, singing, and telling stories. After 66 days on the stormy seas, the ship finally landed at Provincetown. This safe harbor was at the tip of Cape Cod in present-day Massachusetts. The date was November 11, 1620. The Pilgrims had made it to the New World.

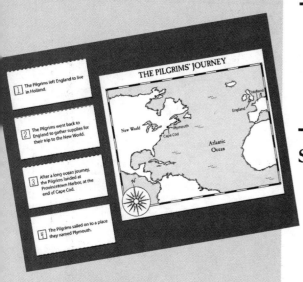

THE PILGRIMS' JOURNEY

Help your students to understand the sequence of moves that the Pilgrims made on their journey to the New World with this map project.

MATERIALS

- page 11, reproduced for each student
- 9" x 12" (23 x 30.5 cm) construction paper
- crayons
- scissors
- glue

STEPS TO FOLLOW

1. Read the story of the Pilgrims' decision to move to the New World to the students. The information that you need to summarize is included on the bottom of this page.
2. Have students cut out and then glue the map on page 11 to the construction paper.
3. Next, read the captions together.
4. Have students number the captions to show the order in which the events happened.
5. Instruct students to cut out the captions and glue them in order next to the map.
6. Help students draw the Pilgrims' path on the map. Use a different color for each part of the journey.

The Pilgrims' decision to leave England was a difficult one. They didn't want to leave their homeland. But they wanted to practice their own religion. In England, this was not allowed.

The Pilgrims left England to live in Holland. Holland was a safer place to practice their beliefs. The Pilgrims did not stay that long. They had a hard time understanding the Dutch language. They had also heard about the New World across the Atlantic Ocean. This is where they would find a new life. The Pilgrims returned to England and gathered supplies for their journey to the New World.

The Pilgrims spent months traveling by ship across the Atlantic Ocean. After a long journey, the Pilgrims landed at Provincetown Harbor, at the end of Cape Cod.

Then the Pilgrims sailed on to a place they called Plymouth. The Pilgrims had found a home in the New World.

THE PILGRIMS' JOURNEY

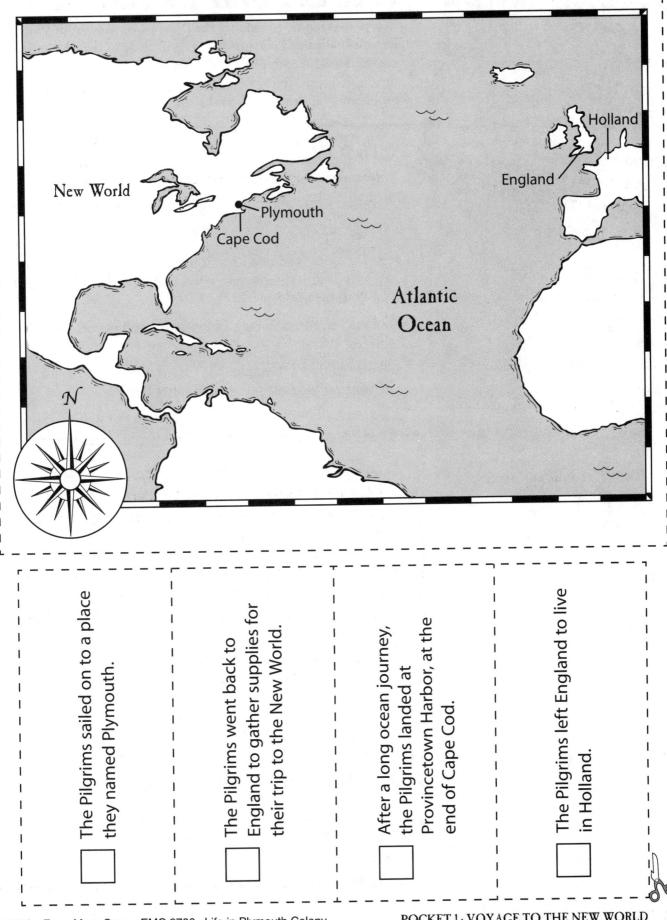

The Pilgrims sailed on to a place they named Plymouth.

☐

The Pilgrims went back to England to gather supplies for their trip to the New World.

☐

After a long ocean journey, the Pilgrims landed at Provincetown Harbor, at the end of Cape Cod.

☐

The Pilgrims left England to live in Holland.

☐

The Mayflower

MAYFLOWER MODEL

Before making this model of the *Mayflower*, draw a line 90 feet long (27 m) on the playground or gym floor so that students can see the actual length of the *Mayflower*. Look at the space allotted for the Pilgrims' living quarters. Discuss with your students the problems of spending 9½ weeks confined to small living quarters.

STEPS TO FOLLOW

1. Show pictures of the *Mayflower* or other ships of that era to the students, if available. Review the information about the ship with students, using the teacher fact sheet and student booklet for reference.

2. Have students color and cut out the *Mayflower* pattern and then glue it to the construction paper. Have students read the facts about the ship.

3. Instruct students to cut out the cross section and cover pieces.

4. Direct students to staple the cross section and then the cover over the bottom section of the ship.

5. Now the students are able to look inside the ship.

MATERIALS

- pages 13 and 14, reproduced for each student
- 9" x 12" (23 x 30.5 cm) blue construction paper
- scissors
- stapler
- glue
- crayons or marking pens
- pictures of the *Mayflower*

MAYFLOWER MODEL

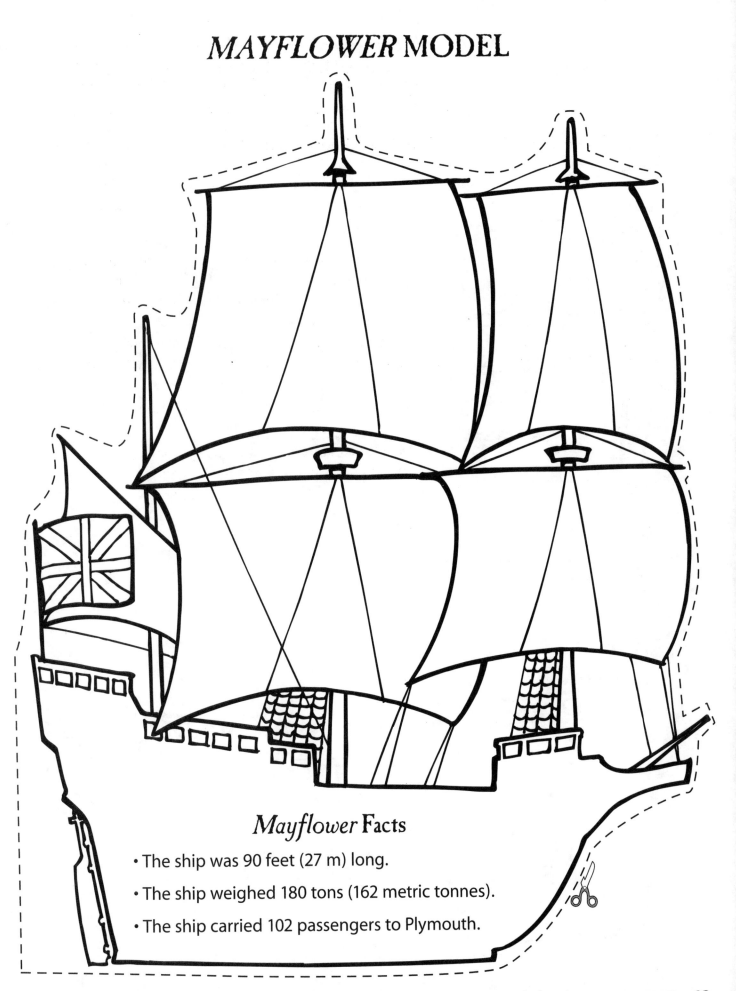

Mayflower Facts

- The ship was 90 feet (27 m) long.
- The ship weighed 180 tons (162 metric tonnes).
- The ship carried 102 passengers to Plymouth.

MAYFLOWER MODEL

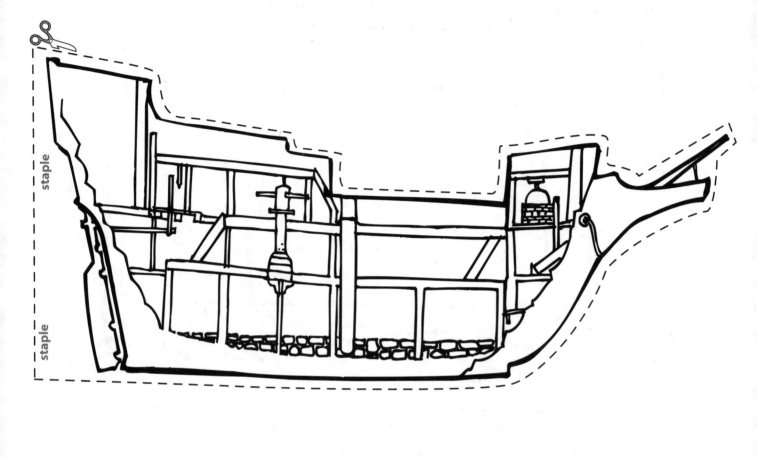

The Mayflower

PACKING FOR THE VOYAGE

fold

Mayflower Voyage

Open up the trunk to
see what I am taking
to the New World.

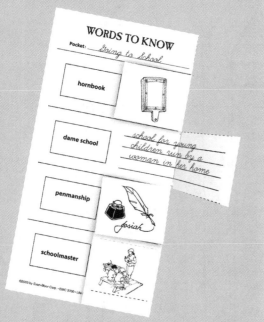

WORDS TO KNOW

As your students learn about life in Plymouth Colony, have them complete this picture dictionary. Four words are added in each pocket. Reproduce page 17 for each student when a new pocket is started.

STEPS TO FOLLOW

As each pocket is studied, guide students through these steps to complete a Words to Know dictionary page.

Step 1

1. Color and cut out the pictures and words found on the pocket label page.

2. Glue the four words into the word boxes on page 17.

3. Guide students in writing a definition of each word.

Step 2

   The Words to Know for each pocket are found in the student booklet.

   After students have read the student booklet, assist them in scanning to find any of the Words to Know. Reread the section containing the word. Help students form a simple definition. (See page 18 for an answer key.) Write the definition on the chalkboard for students to copy. More capable students may be able to write the definitions independently after a few pockets.

Step 4

4. Instruct students to cut on the dotted lines and fold the flaps. Glue the pictures onto the outer flaps.

MATERIALS

- page 17, reproduced for each student
- scissors
- glue
- crayons
- stapler
- pencil

EMC 3700 · Life in Plymouth Colony · ©2003 by Evan-Moor Corp.

WORDS TO KNOW

Pocket: _____

glue word here

glue word here

fold

glue word here

fold

glue word here

fold

WORDS TO KNOW

TEACHER ANSWER KEY

Pocket 1—Voyage to the New World

1. **hardtack** — a hard, dry biscuit
2. **Pilgrim** — a wanderer; member of the English group who founded Plymouth Colony
3. **New World** — the Americas
4. **voyage** — a trip or journey on water

Pocket 2—The New World

1. **compact** — an agreement between people or groups
2. **dugout** — a shelter built partly above and below ground
3. **meetinghouse** — a large building where Pilgrims met
4. **settlement** — a small village

Pocket 3—Building a Village

1. **militia** — an army
2. **musket** — a gun that fired a single shot
3. **town crier** — a man who announced the news to the villagers
4. **village green** — a park in the center of town

Pocket 4—Home Sweet Home

1. **cauldron** — a large iron cooking pot
2. **flint** — a very hard gray stone that sparks when struck
3. **keeping room** — a large open room
4. **settle** — a long wooden bench with high back and sides

Pocket 5—The Family

1. **bubble and squeak** — fish and vegetable stew
2. **breeches** — short pants
3. **doublet** — a man's jacket
4. **waistcoat** — a woman's jacket

Pocket 6—Working in Plymouth Colony

1. **apprentice** — someone who learns a craft by working with a skilled person
2. **craft** — work in which you make things with your hands
3. **craftsperson** — someone skilled at making things with his or her hands
4. **barter** — to trade or exchange goods

Pocket 7—Going to School

1. **dame school** — a school for young children run by a woman in her home
2. **hornbook** — a paddle-shaped writing book
3. **penmanship** — handwriting
4. **schoolmaster** — a male teacher

Pocket 8—What Did the Pilgrims Give Us?

1. **custom** — a tradition; something that is done regularly
2. **manners** — polite behavior
3. **herbs** — plants used in cooking and in some medicines
4. **marketplace** — a place where people buy and sell food or goods

EMC 3700 · Life in Plymouth Colony · ©2003 by Evan-Moor Corp.

Pocket 2
THE NEW WORLD

CUT AND PASTE

See page 2 for information on how to prepare the pocket label. See page 16 for information on how to prepare the "Words to Know" activity.

FACT SHEET

Read the background information to familiarize yourself with the Pilgrims in the New World. Share the information with your students as appropriate. Incorporate library and multimedia resources that are available.

STUDENT BOOKLET

See page 2 for information on how to prepare the student booklet. Read and discuss the information booklet as a class. Encourage students to read their booklets to partners or independently.

ACTIVITIES

Students learn about the Mayflower Compact the Pilgrims wrote and compare it with the rules in the classroom.

The first Thanksgiving was a joyous occasion that lasted three days. The Pilgrims and the Indians had a feast and played games. Students color the picture of the Thanksgiving feast and then complete a word search about the first Thanksgiving.

THE NEW WORLD

©2003 by Evan-Moor Corp. • EMC 3700

WORDS TO KNOW
See page 16 for directions.

settlement

dugout

meetinghouse

The Mayflower Compact

compact

THE NEW WORLD

After the Pilgrims landed, they spent time exploring the area to find a suitable place to live. They chose the land near Plymouth. The Pilgrims were still living on the ship because they had not built any shelters. The "great sickness" was beginning to take its toll among the Pilgrims and the crew of the *Mayflower*. The great sickness was a combination of pneumonia, typhus, and scurvy, which devastated the people. By the end of the first winter, half of the colonists had died, and nearly half of the crew did not survive to make the return trip to England in the spring.

That first winter, when weather permitted, many colonists went ashore and cut down timber to build temporary shelters until permanent houses could be built. The temporary houses were actually dugouts made of sticks and earth built into the side of a hill. The colonists also copied the design of Native American wigwams and used them for shelters. It was agreed that each man should build his own permanent house. They would all cooperate and build a common house where their supplies would be stored. The common house was also called the meetinghouse because it was used as a fort and as a place to pray and talk.

The weather began to clear in March, so the colonists were able to start work on family gardens and their permanent houses. They also planted some of the seeds that they had brought from England. These seeds did not grow well in the rocky soil. These early Pilgrims did not know how to hunt or fish, so food was running low.

A tall Indian arrived three months after the Pilgrims arrived and just in time to help the Pilgrims. The Pilgrims were surprised when the Indian, named Samoset, introduced himself in English. His English was limited, so the next day he brought an older Indian, whose name was Squanto, to help him. Squanto had been in England, so he spoke the English language well. Samoset, an Abnaki Indian, and Squanto, a Patuxet Indian, had been staying with the Wampanoag Indians that lived nearby. Squanto taught the Pilgrims how to find herring, a kind of fish, and how to use it as a fertilizer when planting their seeds. He taught them how to plant corn, pumpkins, and beans. He also taught them how to find clams and eels, and how to hunt for deer, bears, and turkeys. Squanto showed them where to find nuts and berries.

Squanto and Samoset reassured the Wampanoag that the Pilgrims were peaceful. Chief Massasoit of the Wampanoag and 60 of his men came to meet with the leaders of the Pilgrim colony. Following introductory ceremonies, the terms of a peace treaty were agreed to by both parties. Some of the points of the treaty were that whenever they met, they agreed that no Wampanoag would hurt any Pilgrim. If a Wampanoag did injure someone, he would be sent to the Pilgrims for punishment. They both agreed to leave their weapons behind whenever they met. They agreed to be allies. It was the first known treaty of its kind. This peace treaty lasted for 50 years between the Pilgrims and the Wampanoag.

In the fall of 1621, the Pilgrims and the Wampanoag came together in celebration of the fall harvest. For three days, the entire settlement feasted on wild ducks, geese, and turkeys. The Wampanoag also brought five deer for the celebration. For entertainment, there were shooting and bow-and-arrow competitions. There were also footraces and wrestling matches. It was a time of peace and joy. The Pilgrims were thankful that their Indian allies had helped them survive the first year of the settlement in the New World. This was the first Thanksgiving in colonial America.

THE NEW WORLD

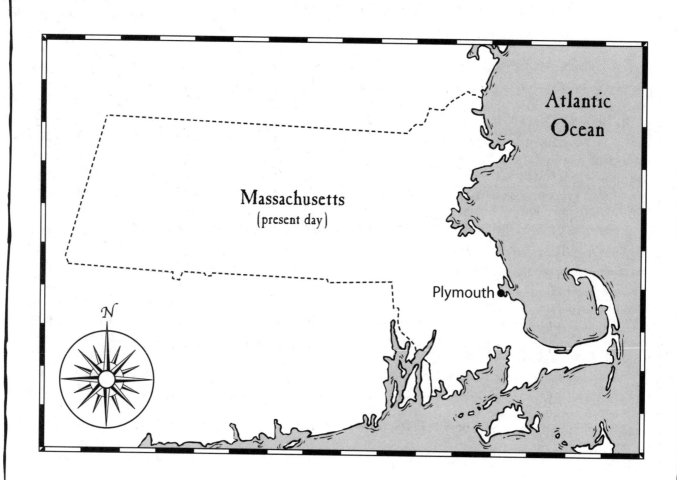

When the Pilgrims landed in the New World, they had to find a good place to live. A group of men found land near a small bay. They called this new **settlement** Plymouth. It was located in the present-day state of Massachusetts. This would be their home in the New World. The Pilgrim men agreed on the rules everyone would follow in Plymouth. They wrote these rules down in the Mayflower **Compact.**

The Pilgrims lived on the ship until they could build homes. They built shelters called dugouts and wigwams at first. **Dugouts** were made of sticks and mud. They were built into the side of a hill. Indian wigwams were round. Wigwams were made of reeds and bark. The Pilgrims spent a cold winter on the ship and in these shelters.

The Pilgrims finished their wooden houses in the spring. They also built a bigger house called the **meetinghouse.** Everybody met there to pray and talk. The people also planted gardens. The seeds did not grow well in the rocky soil. The Pilgrims did not know how to hunt or fish. Food was running out, and the Pilgrims were worried.

Two Indians came to help the Pilgrims. Their names were Samoset and Squanto. They could both speak English. Squanto taught the Pilgrims how to plant corn, pumpkins, and beans. He also showed them how to hunt for deer, bears, and turkeys. The two Indians taught the Pilgrims where to find nuts and berries to eat. The Pilgrims would not have made it through the first year without the help of these new friends.

Squanto and Samoset helped the Pilgrims become friends with the Wampanoag Indian tribe. Chief Massasoit of the Wampanoag made a peace treaty with the Pilgrims. They agreed they would be friends and not fight. The two groups came together to have a harvest celebration. They ate wild ducks, geese, turkeys, and deer. They had footraces and wrestling matches for fun. This was the first Thanksgiving.

THE MAYFLOWER COMPACT

When the Pilgrims landed in Plymouth, the Pilgrim leaders met and wrote an agreement called the Mayflower Compact. They believed that they needed to work together in order to succeed. The Pilgrim men agreed on the laws that they would follow, and 41 men signed the compact. Then they voted to have John Carver be governor of the new colony.

STEPS TO FOLLOW

1. Using the information in the introductory paragraph, tell students what the Mayflower Compact was and why it was written.

2. Distribute page 26 to students. Together, read the simplified ideas contained in the Mayflower Compact.

3. Have students glue the compact onto construction paper and cut around the edges to make a border.

4. Compare the Mayflower Compact with your class rules. Discuss with your students how rules that all class members must follow help to guarantee a well-functioning community.

The Mayflower Compact
November 1620

We, the Pilgrims of the Mayflower, promise to have fair rules in our new colony of Plymouth. The men will choose a leader for the colony. He will be called the governor. We promise to obey the new governor of Plymouth.

Signed,

William Bradford
John Carver

MATERIALS

- page 26, reproduced for each student
- 9" x 12" (23 x 30.5 cm) construction paper
- scissors
- glue

The Mayflower Compact

November 1620

We, the Pilgrims of the Mayflower, promise to have fair rules in our new colony of Plymouth. The men will choose a leader for the colony. He will be called the governor. We promise to obey the new governor of Plymouth.

Signed,

William Bradford
John Carver

EMC 3700 · Life in Plymouth Colony · ©2003 by Evan-Moor Corp.

THE FIRST THANKSGIVING

The first Thanksgiving was held in October 1621. This three-day harvest celebration included 52 English colonists and 91 Wampanoag Indians. The colonists were grateful to the Indians for helping them survive the first year. In English style, Chief Massasoit and his leaders ate with the leading men of the colony at a "high table," which probably featured the best foods. Tables were set up both indoors and outdoors for the other guests.

When people think of a traditional Thanksgiving dinner, they think of such foods as roasted turkey, mashed potatoes and gravy, sweet potatoes, cranberry sauce, and pumpkin pie. Students will be surprised to learn the other kinds of foods included when the Pilgrims and the Indians had their harvest feast together.

Students color a picture of the Pilgrim and then complete a word search of foods served at the first Thanksgiving.

STEPS TO FOLLOW

1. Discuss the background information about the first Thanksgiving with students.

2. Distribute page 28 and have students color the picture.

3. Discuss the kinds of foods eaten by the Pilgrims and the Wampanoag. Then have students complete the word search.

MATERIALS

- page 28, reproduced for each student
- pencil
- crayons

THE FIRST THANKSGIVING

```
C A B B A G E S A B L J Y S
X Y A C D G E E S E D E S T
O Y S T E R S S A B U D E R
B D E F N G E A L C C T D A
C F X R Y H Z L O P K U Q W
L E O S S R U B B A S R S B
A C D I E Z Y L S O L N P E
M M D E E R R P T E E I B R
S A B S S R I P E O E P O R
R T U R K E Y S R Y L S X I
Z Y L J V K U E S F S W J E
A C H P U M P K I N S G F S
G O O S E B E R R I E S U T
```

Word Box

cabbages	lobsters
clams	oysters
corn	pumpkins
deer	radishes
ducks	strawberries
eels	turkeys
geese	turnips
gooseberries	

EMC 3700 · Life in Plymouth Colony · ©2003 by Evan-Moor Corp.

Pocket 3

BUILDING A VILLAGE

CUT AND PASTE

Pocket Label, Words to Know . . . . **page 30**
See page 2 for information on how to prepare
the pocket label. See page 16 for information on
how to prepare the "Words to Know" activity.

FACT SHEET

Building a Village . . . . **page 31**
Read the background information to familiarize
yourself with the way Pilgrims built a village.
Share the information with your students as
appropriate. Incorporate library and multimedia
resources that are available.

STUDENT BOOKLET

Building a Village Booklet . . . . **pages 32–34**
See page 2 for information on how to prepare
the student booklet. Read and discuss the
information booklet as a class. Encourage
students to read their booklets to partners or
independently.

ACTIVITIES

The Town Crier . . . . **pages 35 & 36**
The town crier's job was to announce important
news to the villagers. Students pretend they
have that job in the village. They write a news
bulletin and then announce it to the class.

The Tithing Man . . . . **page 37**
During Sunday religious services, the tithing
man's job was to watch to make sure people
were listening attentively to the sermon.
Students make a model of the tithing man's fur
stick that he used to tickle the noses of sleepy
parishioners.

BUILDING A VILLAGE

WORDS TO KNOW

See page 16 for directions.

musket

militia

town crier

village green

FACT SHEET
BUILDING A VILLAGE

For the first 10 years, the colony of New Plymouth had only one settlement, the village, or town, of Plymouth. For the first two years, the Pilgrims built their homes and a common meetinghouse. Next, the design of the town called for a palisade, a strong fence, to be built around the town's edge. This palisade was built of split logs. Inside the fence was enough room for 12 family homes and gardens. The Pilgrims also built a fort at the top of the hill and placed the cannon from the *Mayflower* at the fort.

As the village grew, more and more buildings were constructed. Streets were dirt paths, but a general design of a village was taking shape. The village had a blacksmith shop, an inn or tavern, a schoolhouse, a general store, a sawmill, and a flour mill. The center of the village became a park called the village green. This was an open area where cattle grazed and children played. Eventually, more shops and businesses grew as the need for them increased.

A man called the town crier announced news in the village. He walked along the village paths, ringing a bell or banging on a drum. This prompted people to meet on the village green to hear the local news. He would announce that a new shipment of supplies had just arrived or that a new law had just been made. News was also received in the form of letters. There was no regular mail service. People paid a man to deliver their letters in the village and to the surrounding farmland and other settlements. It could take up to a month to receive a letter this way. Letters were sent back to England by sailing ships.

The Pilgrims missed their families and friends back in England. In fact, they were so lonesome, they called their new home New England. They continued to obey English laws and the Mayflower Compact they had drawn up when they first landed. There was no book of laws until 1636. Until then, the appointed governor could do what he wanted as long as he did not go against the laws of England.

As the colony grew, a more complicated system of government was developed. There was a governor and a group of magistrates who made up the General Court. The "freemen" of the colony (wealthy men over the age of 30) elected them. Only about one-third of the adult males in the colony were considered freemen. The General Court met four times a year. It was responsible for taxing the colonists, making laws, and hearing court cases. The most common cases were disputes over property. Most of the serious crimes were punished by banishment from the colony. For lesser crimes, such as drunkenness, a public whipping or a public apology was ordered.

It was the law in the village that people had to attend church services on Sunday. Every Sunday the villagers were summoned to the meetinghouse by a drum. The militia marched up the road, followed by the governor and the preacher. The rest of the village followed. There were two services, and everyone was required to attend both. There was a dinner served between services. The reading of the Bible and the preacher's sermon were always included in the services. No one was allowed to work on Sunday. This was the Sabbath day.

Plymouth had its own militia. A militia was a loosely formed army. Males between the ages of 16 and 60 had to join. Once a month, the men would have to practice marching and shooting. Men in the militia carried guns, swords, and knives to protect the villagers from unfriendly Native American tribes.

The village of Plymouth was a bustling place that continued to grow and prosper after the humble beginnings of its first settlers.

Note: Reproduce pages 32–34 for students to use with the "Building a Village Booklet" activity, as described on page 29.

BUILDING A VILLAGE

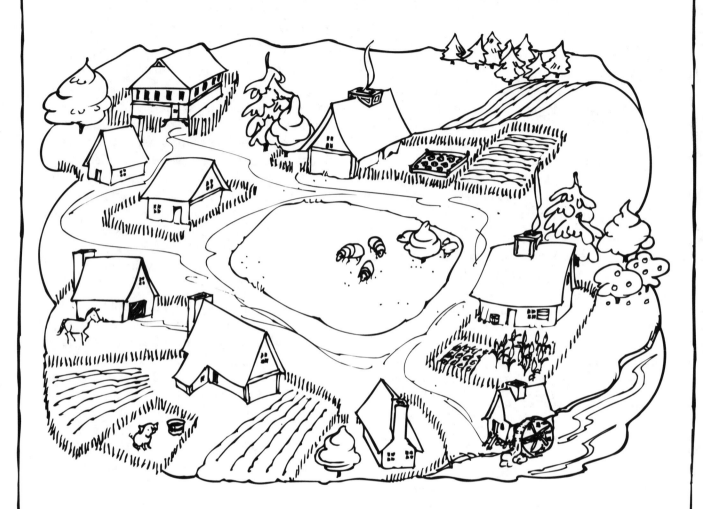

The first Pilgrims built a village in Plymouth. The village had houses with gardens around them. There was a meetinghouse and a general store. There were stores like the blacksmith's shop and the carpenter's shop. There was a village green in the center of town. The **village green** was like a park. As more Pilgrims moved to Plymouth, the village grew bigger.

A man called the **town crier** announced the news in the village. He walked along the paths, ringing a bell or banging on a drum. This meant that everybody was to meet in the village green. He would then tell everybody the news. People in the village liked to write letters to tell about the news of the village. Letters were sent back to family and friends in England by sailing ships.

The village had rules. Everybody had to pay taxes. Everybody had to go to church on Sunday. The governor of the village held court four times a year. If people broke the law, the governor would punish them. If a Pilgrim did something bad like hurting another person, he had to leave Plymouth and never return. If a person did something wrong like stealing, that person might have been whipped in public. He would also have to apologize to all the villagers.

Plymouth had its own militia. A **militia** was an army. All men between the ages of 16 and 60 had to join. Once a month, the men would practice marching and shooting. The men carried heavy **muskets** and swords. The men kept the village safe. Another job for the militia was to march the villagers to the meetinghouse every Sunday for church services.

Everybody went to the meetinghouse on Sundays for two church services. The preacher read from the Bible and gave a sermon. The sermon was a long speech about following the teachings in the Bible. There was a dinner between the two services. Sundays were not for work. Sundays were only for prayer and giving thanks. The Pilgrims were thankful for their village and for a new beginning in a New World.

THE TOWN CRIER

Students become town criers and announce important news to the other "settlers" in your classroom.

STEPS TO FOLLOW

1. Have students color and cut out the picture of the town crier on page 36. Talk about the job the town crier had in the village. (See page 33.)

2. Instruct students to fold the construction paper in half and glue the picture to the front. Trim the construction paper so that a narrow border shows around the picture.

3. Have students think about what types of news the town crier might have announced. List examples on the chalkboard or a chart, using the teacher fact sheet for reference.

4. Direct students to create and write a script for a town crier on the writing form on page 36. You may want to do this as a class and have students copy the results from the chalkboard.

5. Then have students cut out and glue the script to the inside of the town crier booklet.

6. Take advantage of this opportunity for dramatic reading. Students can stand at the front of the class and pretend to be a town crier, reading their scripts with feeling. Before they read the script, you may want to allow them to use a bell to announce their arrival.

MATERIALS

- page 36, reproduced for each student
- 9" x 12" (23 x 30.5 cm) construction paper
- fine-tip marking pens or crayons
- pencil
- glue
- scissors
- Optional: school bell

THE TOWN CRIER

EMC 3700 · Life in Plymouth Colony · ©2003 by Evan-Moor Corp.

THE TITHING MAN

Students read about the role of the tithing man and make a model of his pole for their pockets.

STEPS TO FOLLOW

1. Have students put a bit of glue on one end of the dowel and fit it into the hole in the wooden bead. Let the glue dry completely.

2. Use a glue gun to attach a "tail" of fur to the other end of each student's dowel.

3. Read the information about the tithing man with your students.

4. Have them cut out and glue the information to the construction paper to make a tag, punch a hole in the tag, and then tie the tag to the pole model with a piece of yarn.

MATERIALS

- page 37, information section reproduced for each student
- 3" x 5" (7.5 x 13 cm) black construction paper
- 12" (30.5 cm) wooden dowel or chopstick
- scrap of fake fur
- large wooden bead (the hole should be the same circumference as the dowel or chopstick)
- glue
- glue gun
- hole punch
- yarn
- scissors

THE TITHING MAN

Sunday services in Plymouth Colony were long. Children had to sit quietly and listen. If a baby fell asleep during the Sunday service, no one cared. But if an older child or an adult fell asleep, the church watchman, or tithing man, woke them. He carried a long pole. On one end of the pole was a furry fox or squirrel tail. On the other end was a wooden knob. If children talked or giggled, the tithing man tapped them on the head with the knob. If listeners fell asleep, the tithing man tickled their noses with the furry tail. Adults who smiled or whispered during the services had to pay a fine.

Pocket 4

HOME SWEET HOME

CUT AND PASTE

Pocket Label, Words to Know . . . . **page 39**
See page 2 for information on how to prepare
the pocket label. See page 16 for information on
how to prepare the "Words to Know" activity.

FACT SHEET

Home Sweet Home . . . . **page 40**
Read the background information to familiarize
yourself with the home life of the Pilgrims.
Share the information with your students as
appropriate. Incorporate library and multimedia
resources that are available.

STUDENT BOOKLET

Home Sweet Home Booklet . . . . **pages 41–43**
See page 2 for information on how to prepare
the student booklet. Read and discuss the
information booklet as a class. Encourage
students to read their booklets to partners or
independently.

ACTIVITY

A Keeping Room Diorama . . . . **pages 44–47**
Students learn about the keeping room
when they make a folding model of this most
important room in the house.

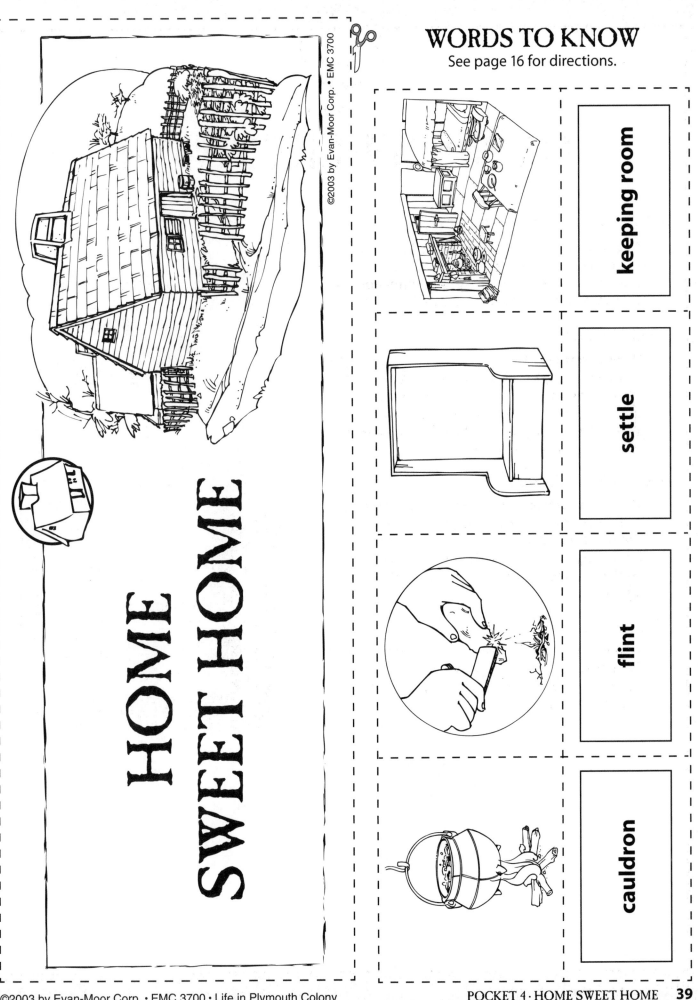

WORDS TO KNOW

See page 16 for directions.

keeping room

settle

flint

cauldron

HOME SWEET HOME

©2003 by Evan-Moor Corp. • EMC 3700

HOME SWEET HOME

The Pilgrims built their homes either in the village or in the surrounding countryside. Village homes consisted of a house and a garden. The country homesteads consisted of a house, barn, garden, pen for the animals, and fields.

Houses were built out of timbers cut into beams. The beams were nailed over a frame. The frame was made from thin slats of wood glued together with a thick paste. The paste was a mixture of straw, sand, and water. The Pilgrims called the frame "wattle" and the paste "daub." Windows were small openings. They were covered with a waxed paper because glass had to be imported from England and that was very expensive. The first roofs were thatched. Thatched roofs were made from reeds. By 1627 a law was passed that colonists could not make thatched roofs anymore because they burned so easily. The Pilgrims' started making wood-shingle roofs after that.

The inside of the houses was very plain. The walls of sturdier homes were made of whitewashed plaster over a lathe of sticks. Behind the sticks were straw and dried moss to keep heat from escaping. If the family could afford it, they had sawed wooden planks for floors. Most Pilgrims' homes had dirt or stone floors.

The house had one large open room with a huge fireplace in the middle of the room, and a small storage room off to the side. The large open room was called the keeping room. The family cooked, ate, worked, and slept in the keeping room. The fireplace was used for heating and cooking. The small storage room was called the buttery. This was where dried vegetables and cured meat were stored.

Most Pilgrims had plain furniture. There was a long wooden table. The family sat on wooden stools, or they sat together on the settle. The settle was a long wooden bench with high sides and a high back. The parents got to sleep on a real bed off the floor. The bed was short and hard. There were curtains around it for privacy. The children slept on folded-up mattresses kept in the corner of the keeping room. The mattresses were filled with straw, feathers, or bits of wool. Sometimes older children were allowed to sleep on the overhead rafters in the buttery. The babies slept in wooden cradles near the fireplace.

The huge fireplace and chimney provided the Pilgrims' only heat and cooking source. Giant logs kept the blaze going. The logs were so big that it took two horses to drag the gigantic logs into the house. It was almost a full-time job chopping logs and keeping the fire going at all times. When the fire died down, kindling had to be added. If that did not work, the family had to use flint to make a spark. There were no matches in the early days of colonial America.

There was no running water, so it had to be fetched from the spring in wooden buckets several times a day. If hot water was needed, it was heated in a big cauldron over the fire. Hot water was used to make tea, wash dishes and clothes, and for the occasional bath.

Lighting the house was even a bigger problem than heating it. There were small windows covered with the waxed paper, so the house was dark even in the daytime. Oil lamps, called rushlights, were used at night if the family could afford them. Families mostly gathered around the fireplace to read and work since it provided at least some light.

The harsh New England weather made maintaining a colonial home a real chore. Even though keeping up the home was difficult, the Pilgrims enjoyed their "home sweet home."

 EMC 3700 · Life in Plymouth Colony · ©2003 by Evan-Moor Corp.

Note: Reproduce pages 41–43 for students to use with the "Home Sweet Home Booklet" activity, as described on page 38.

HOME SWEET HOME

The Pilgrims built wooden houses. First, the men cut thin pieces of wood and glued them together with daub. Daub was a thick paste made from water, sand, and straw. The glued pieces of wood made a frame called a wattle. The men nailed cut logs to the wattle frame. The Pilgrims made roofs with wood shingles. They cut out one or two windows and covered them with a waxed paper.

The inside of the houses was very plain. They had thin walls where tools were hung. The floors were made of dirt, stone, or wood. There was one large room called the **keeping room.** The family ate, worked, and slept in that room. There was a large fireplace in the middle of the room. There was also a small storage area called the buttery.

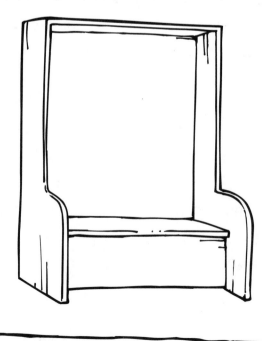

The Pilgrims did not have much furniture. The family ate at a long wooden table. They sat on wooden stools or on the settle. The **settle** was a wooden bench with high sides and a high back. The parents slept in a hard bed with a curtain around it. The children slept on straw or feather mattresses on the floor. Babies slept in wooden cradles near the fireplace.

The fireplace was very important to the family. The huge fireplace was used for cooking and for warmth. Giant logs kept the fire going. The Pilgrims did not have matches. They lit the fire using a flint. **Flint** is a hard stone that makes a spark when you hit it. All day the family added pieces of wood so the fire would not go out.

There was no running water in the houses. The Pilgrims had to take wooden buckets to the stream to get water. They heated the water in a big **cauldron** over the fire. Hot water was used to make tea and soups. The women used hot water to wash dishes and clothes. Pilgrims used hot water to take baths. The family had many chores to do to keep the house in good shape.

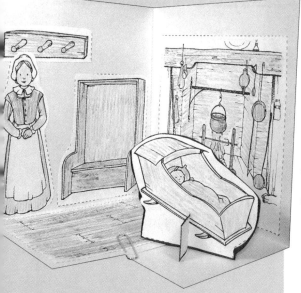

A KEEPING ROOM DIORAMA

Students make this folding model of the keeping room. Encourage them to add details and furniture of their own as they read about the type of homes in Plymouth Colony.

STEPS TO FOLLOW

1. Review the meaning of the keeping room with students, using the information from the teacher fact sheet and student booklet.

2. Help students make the diorama following the directions below.

How to Make the Diorama

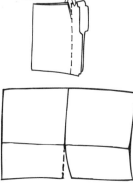

a. Make a 2" (5 cm) vertical cut off a folded file folder as shown.

b. Open up the file folder and cut a 4½" (11.5 cm) slit on the fold.

c. Fold up the two sides to create the floor of the keeping room. They can paper-clip the folded sides in the center to create a diorama.

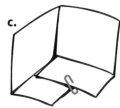

MATERIALS

- pages 45–47, reproduced on light-colored construction paper for each student
- old file folder
- crayons or marking pens
- glue
- paper clip
- scissors

3. Have students add items to the diorama following the directions below.

How to Add Pictures

a. Color and cut out the patterns on pages 45–47.

b. Glue the pictures to the diorama as follows:
  - cover—title, boy, barrel
  - inside left—girl, clothes pegs, settle, wooden floor
  - inside right—fireplace

c. Make the stand-up cradle.
  - Slip the stand-up tab onto the cradle at the slit. Fold the tab back to make the cradle stand.

4. The cradle should be unfolded and placed inside the flattened file folder for storage in the pocket.

A Keeping Room

EMC 3700 · Life in Plymouth Colony · ©2003 by Evan-Moor Corp.

A Keeping Room

A KEEPING ROOM DIORAMA

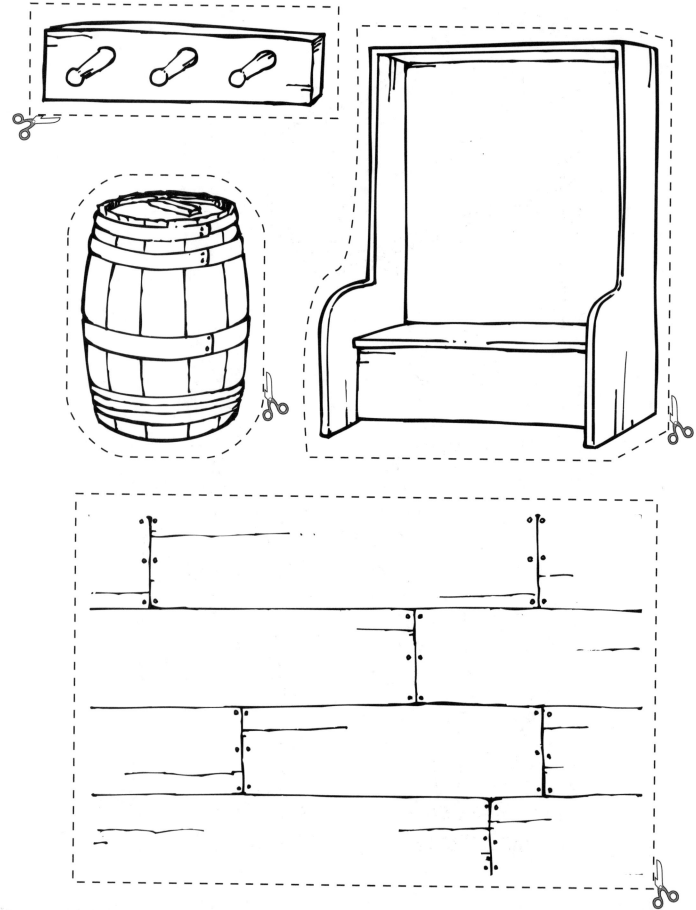

EMC 3700 · Life in Plymouth Colony · ©2003 by Evan-Moor Corp.

A KEEPING ROOM DIORAMA

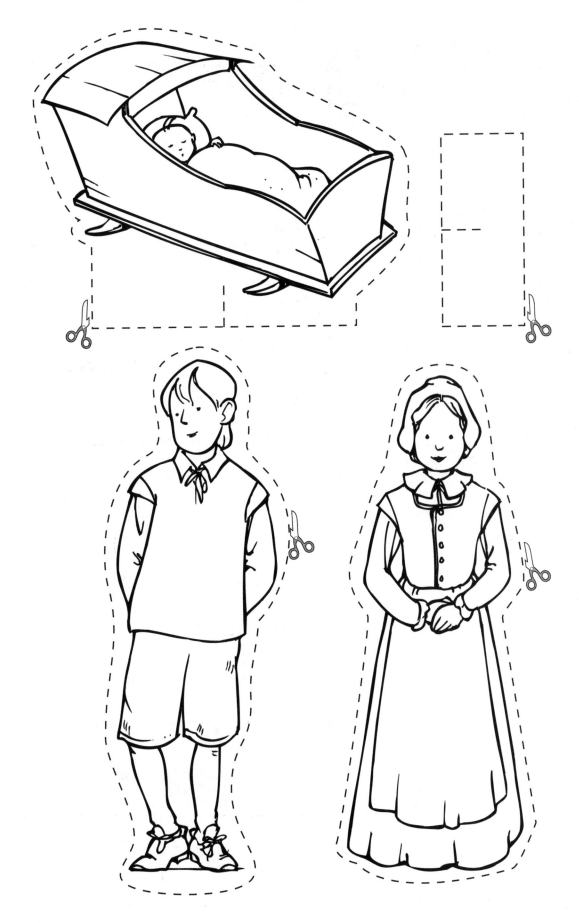

THE FAMILY

CUT AND PASTE

Pocket Label, Words to Know .... **page 49**
See page 2 for information on how to prepare
the pocket label. See page 16 for information on
how to prepare the "Words to Know" activity.

FACT SHEET

The Family .... **page 50**
Read the background information to familiarize
yourself with family life in Plymouth. Share the
information with your students as appropriate.
Incorporate library and multimedia resources
that are available.

STUDENT BOOKLET

The Family Booklet .... **pages 51–53**
See page 2 for information on how to prepare
the student booklet. Read and discuss the
information booklet as a class. Encourage
students to read their booklets to partners or
independently.

ACTIVITIES

Table Manners .... **pages 54–56**
Colonial children had to follow strict rules of
behavior at family dinners. Students make a
"cast-iron pot" filled with a "fish stew" of
manners.

Pilgrim Puppets .... **pages 57–59**
In this activity, students make Pilgrim puppets
to learn about colonial clothing styles.

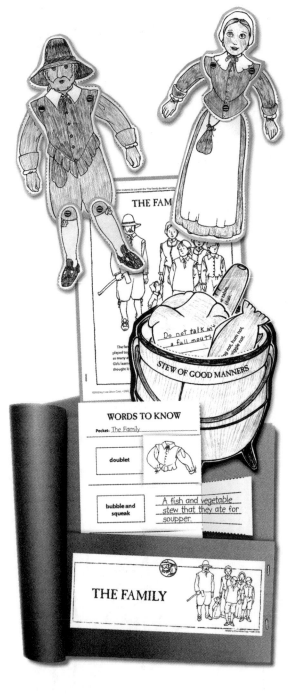

THE FAMILY

WORDS TO KNOW

See page 16 for directions.

breeches

doublet

waistcoat

bubble and squeak

THE FAMILY

The Pilgrims usually had large families. They had from 2 to 15 children. Pilgrim families lived and worked closely together. Parents passed on their way of life to their children. Boys learned from their fathers how to farm, and girls learned domestic skills from their mothers. When a young man was about the age of 23, he asked for his parents' permission to marry. As a gift, he was given a piece of the family's land.

The Pilgrim family worked and played together. Pilgrim parents believed that their most important duty was to raise their children to be respectful and to worship God. Parents were strict, and children were expected to honor and obey their parents. Discipline was often quite harsh. The children were also supposed to have good manners.

The Pilgrims believed that being respectful also meant that they should all wear simple, plain clothes. Both men and women usually had two outfits. One was for daily use and the other for Sunday or a special occasion. The clothes were dark green and black, which were considered respectful colors for church.

Men wore long white cotton shirts and breeches. Breeches were trousers that ran to just below the knee. They put on long woolen stockings that were held up by garters tied above the knee. They added a doublet, which was a jacket, over the white cotton shirt. Men wore dark felt or woolen hats and simple leather shoes.

Women usually wore long cotton shirts and skirts. There were three petticoats under the skirts. They also wore aprons over the skirts. They put on waistcoats over the shirts. Clothes did not have pockets sewn in. The pockets were cloth pouches that were tied to the waist. Women wore coifs on their heads and the same simple leather shoes men wore.

Children dressed like their parents after the age of 7. Before the age of 7, boys and girls wore simple cotton dressing gowns with ties at the shoulder. Parents could grab ahold of those ties to keep children from getting away. Children went barefoot in warmer weather and wore simple leather shoes in the winter.

The family ate simple meals together. They ate only things they could grow or raise. Every family had a garden that provided them with cabbages, turnips, leeks, parsnips, onions, carrots, and radishes. They got their milk, butter, and cheese from their dairy cattle. Pigs provided bacon and ham for special occasions. They gathered wild strawberries, blueberries, raspberries, gooseberries, and blackberries. The Pilgrims also fished for cod, eels, and herring. They fished for shellfish, mussels, and lobsters, but these foods were less popular with the Pilgrims.

No one could have breakfast until the early morning chores were finished. Chores included feeding the animals, milking the cows, fetching the water, and making sure the fire was burning in the fireplace. Breakfast was usually hasty pudding, which was cornmeal porridge.

A typical midday meal consisted of a fish and vegetable stew called bubble and squeak. The family ate home-baked bread made of cornmeal, rye, and barley flour. At night, they may have eaten more hasty pudding or fish stew. The Pilgrims were happy that they could drink the fresh water. Back in England, they drank beer because they feared diseases from the polluted rivers and wells.

After a long workday, the family gathered around the fire to read from the Bible and tell stories before going to bed. The family was very important to the Pilgrims.

EMC 3700 • Life in Plymouth Colony • ©2003 by Evan-Moor Corp.

Note: Reproduce pages 51–53 for students to use with the "The Family Booklet" activity, as described on page 48.

THE FAMILY

The family was important to the Pilgrims. They worked and played together. Pilgrims had large families. Parents sometimes had as many as 15 children. Boys learned how to farm from their fathers. Girls learned how to cook and sew from their mothers. Parents thought it was important to raise honest and hardworking children.

Pilgrim parents also believed children should honor and respect them. They loved their children, but they were very strict. Pilgrims liked their families to have good table manners. The family read a book of manners. One rule in the book was "Stuff not thy mouth to fill thy cheeks." That meant it was not polite to take big bites of food. It was not even polite to talk at the dinner table.

The family ate many vegetables such as cabbages, turnips, leeks, and onions. They raised cows for their milk, butter, and cheese. They ate fish such as cod and herring and even eels. For breakfast they ate hasty pudding. Hasty pudding was cornmeal porridge. For supper they ate **bubble and squeak.** That was a fish and vegetable stew.

The Pilgrims wore plain clothes. They only had two outfits. Men wore long white cotton shirts and dark-colored breeches. **Breeches** were pants that came just below the knee. The men wore a jacket called a **doublet.** They wore woolen socks, leather shoes, and woolen hats. Boys wore the same kind of clothes as their fathers.

Women and girls made all the family's clothing. The women and girls wore long cotton shirts, skirts, and aprons. They put on jackets called **waistcoats.** Women wore cloth pouches tied to their waists as pockets. They wore bonnets called coifs. Young children wore cotton dresses with ties at the shoulder. Parents could grab ahold of those ties to keep the little children from getting away.

TABLE MANNERS

Colonial children had to follow strict rules of behavior, especially at the dinner table. Students make a "cast-iron pot" filled with a "fish stew" of manners.

STEPS TO FOLLOW

1. Have students color the cast-iron pot pattern on page 55 dark gray. Then have students cut it out.

2. Have a helper carefully cut a slit along the dotted line near the top of the pot.

3. Direct students to glue the outer edges of pot to the black construction paper.

4. Have students cut around the pot pattern, leaving a border of black construction paper.

5. Distribute page 56 to students. Read and discuss the manners that are written on the fish and vegetables. Then on the cabbage pattern, students write one rule they have to follow at their own family dinners.

6. Have students color and cut out the fish, carrot, cabbage, and radish pieces.

7. Students slip the fish and vegetables into their pots to make a "stew of good manners."

MATERIALS

- pages 55 and 56, reproduced for each student
- 9" x 12" (23 x 30.5 cm) black construction paper
- pencil
- crayons or colored pencils
- scissors
- glue

EMC 3700 • Life in Plymouth Colony • ©2003 by Evan-Moor Corp.

TABLE MANNERS

(cut to make a slit)

STEW OF GOOD MANNERS

TABLE MANNERS

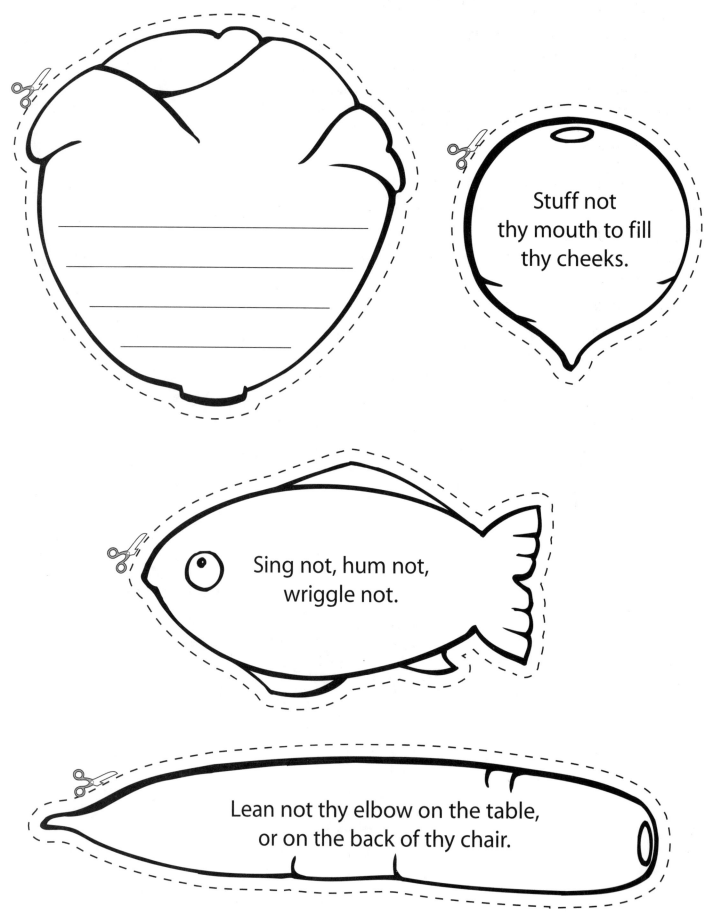

Stuff not
thy mouth to fill
thy cheeks.

Sing not, hum not,
wriggle not.

Lean not thy elbow on the table,
or on the back of thy chair.

PILGRIM PUPPETS

When pictures are shown of the Pilgrims, they are usually dressed in drab-colored clothing, buckled shoes, and hats with buckles. In reality, the Pilgrims wore a lot of earth-colored clothing. Men's doublets and women's waistcoats were shades of red, yellow, blue, or purple, as well as the traditional browns and grays. Men and boys usually wore felt hats with a braided rope as decoration, not buckles. Men and women wore shoes that were plain and made of leather. Men and boys also wore leather boots. Students create movable puppets to show the clothing of the Pilgrims.

STEPS TO FOLLOW

1. Discuss the clothing of the Pilgrims, using the information found in this pocket.

2. Have students color and cut out the puppet pieces.

3. Students then glue the puppet parts to the tagboard to make them sturdier. Allow time for the glue to dry completely.

4. Direct students to carefully cut out the puppet parts.

5. Students attach the parts using paper fasteners, and then tape each puppet to a craft stick.

6. Have students use the puppets to talk to each other about the kinds of clothing they wore in Plymouth. The students could also use the puppets to help them reread the student booklets to partners.

MATERIALS

- pages 58 and 59, reproduced for each student
- 2 craft sticks
- 7 paper fasteners
- crayons or marking pens
- tagboard
- transparent tape
- glue
- scissors

PILGRIM PUPPETS

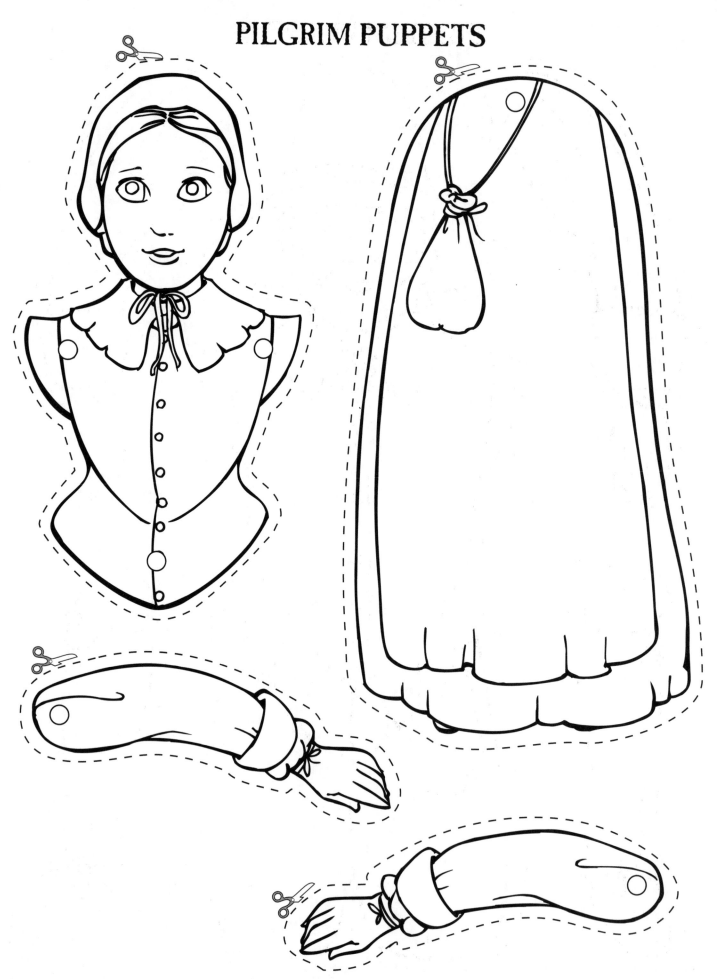

PILGRIM PUPPETS

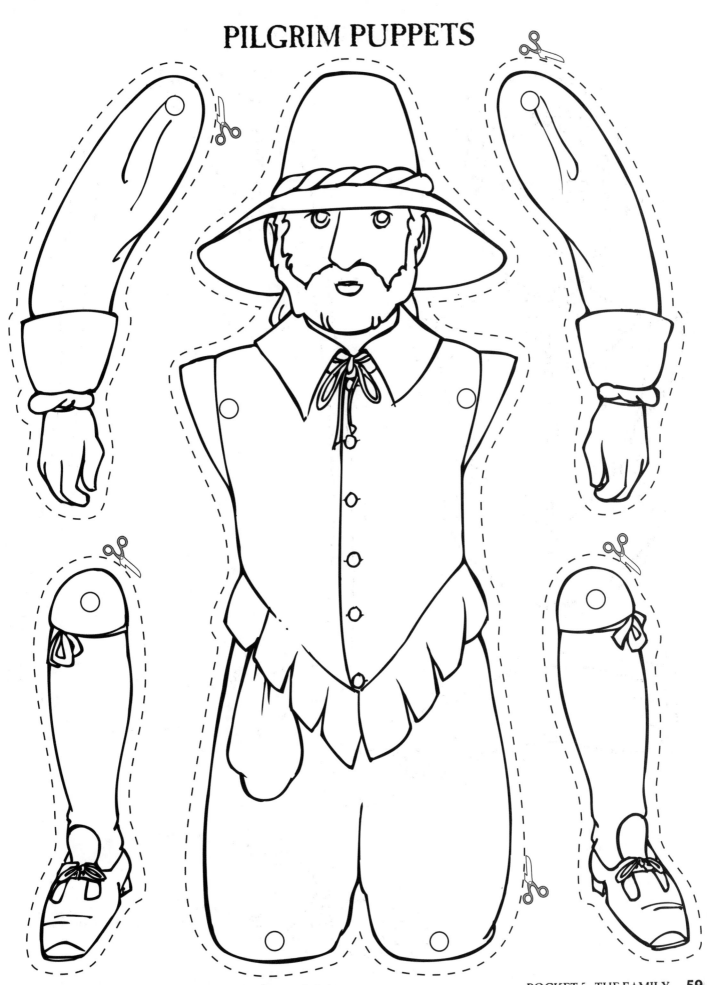

Pocket 6

WORKING IN PLYMOUTH COLONY

CUT AND PASTE

See page 2 for information on how to prepare the pocket label. See page 16 for information on how to prepare the "Words to Know" activity.

FACT SHEET

Read the background information to familiarize yourself with work in Plymouth Colony. Share the information with your students as appropriate. Incorporate library and multimedia resources that are available.

STUDENT BOOKLET

See page 2 for information on how to prepare the student booklet. Read and discuss the information booklet as a class. Encourage students to read their booklets to partners or independently.

ACTIVITIES

There were mostly farmers in early Plymouth. As the years passed, more craftspeople were needed. Students read about eight of these skilled workers in Plymouth as they make job cards about them. Then the students decide which one interests them the most.

Following the directions on page 66, students make a sign to advertise what kind of shop they own.

Students learn about how women created beautiful quilts. Then the students create a special book of historical and original quilt patterns.

WORKING
IN PLYMOUTH COLONY

WORDS TO KNOW
See page 16 for directions.

barter

craftsperson

craft

apprentice

WORKING IN PLYMOUTH COLONY

Most early Pilgrims were farmers. When they arrived in the New England area, they discovered clean air, rich forests, and fresh drinking water. They felt blessed to be able to work the land. Despite the abundant resources, the Pilgrim farmers managed only to grow enough food to feed their own families. The soil was too thin and rocky to do large-scale farming. They did not become wealthy like the Virginia tobacco farmers did. The Pilgrims believed that their farmland should be passed down to the sons of the family. The land was divided into smaller and smaller plots as each generation took over from the last.

The Pilgrim settlers had to turn to crafts and trading to make a living. The Pilgrims sometimes sent their children off to learn a trade at the age of 13. It was more common for boys to live with relatives or friends in larger settlements to learn a trade. They were apprentices for many years, learning to be carpenters, blacksmiths, and tanners. Some girls were "bound out" by their parents to be servants for wealthy families in larger settlements. Some girls learned to be seamstresses and cooks.

Every village had craftspeople who made tools, home furnishings, and other equipment. Families realized it was easier to buy some goods than to make all their own clothing and tools. Blacksmiths were one of the most needed craftspeople. They made everything that could be made of iron. This included weapons, nails, horseshoes, and cooking utensils. Carpenters built wooden items such as furniture and wagons. The cooper was important because he built storage barrels that everyone needed. The miller ground the grain into flour.

Craftspeople made life easier for the settlers, and as time went on, the artisans became more specialized. The hornsmith designed buttons and combs, and the cobbler made and repaired the shoes. The printer published the news, and the postrider delivered the mail. The silversmith made beautiful candlesticks and utensils, and the tinker repaired tin pots and pans.

By the early 1700s, New England shipwrights became important craftspeople. Young men would leave the Plymouth settlement to go work in the shipbuilding business in the new towns of Boston and Salem, Massachusetts. Shipbuilding was a complex craft. There were as many as 30 different kinds of craftsmen building and repairing the sailing ships.

Besides shipbuilding, young men turned to fishing and trading to earn a living in New England. Farmers regularly made the trip north to Boston to sell their cattle, lumber, and grain. These goods were shipped to Europe and the Caribbean. In return, the Pilgrims traded for things like tobacco and European imports to take back to their colony.

While men worked in the fields or part time as craftsmen, the women remained at home. They were highly skilled farmers and craftspeople in their own right. They tended the family gardens and looked after the farm animals. They made all the clothing and bedding for the family. They made soap and candles. They cooked over open fires and preserved all the food for winter. They did all this while still caring for the children.

Children worked hard from the time they were very young. Younger children picked berries or fed the chickens. By the time children were 6, they were given more responsibility. They gathered wood, cleaned the fireplace, fetched the water, and cared for the younger children. Older boys helped plant and harvest the crops. They learned to hunt, fish, and trap. Older girls learned how to make soap, cook, and sew. At age 13, the children were treated as adults and were expected to learn a trade.

Men, women, and children all worked hard. That hard-work ethic will always be associated with the Pilgrims of Plymouth.

WORKING IN PLYMOUTH COLONY

Most people in Plymouth Colony were farmers. They grew corn, wheat, and rye. Those grains gave them the cornmeal and flour they needed for cooking. They raised cows, pigs, sheep, and chickens. That way they could have milk, meat, wool, and eggs. The family worked from 4:00 a.m. until they went to bed at 8:00 p.m. Everybody in the family had to help.

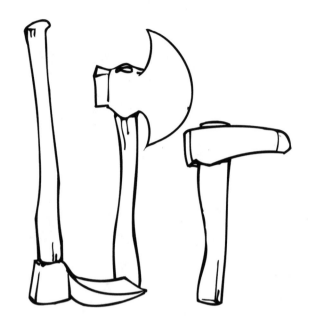

The men planted the crops in the fields. They chopped the wood and built the houses and barns. They made the furniture. The men had to make and fix all their tools. They had to repair the fences around the farm often. Fathers taught their sons how to be farmers. When the sons got older, fathers gave them some of the land to farm.

Women were in charge of the garden and the farm animals. They spun the wool to make cloth, and sewed all the clothes and bedding for the family. They even made their own soap and candles. They turned milk into butter and cheese. The meat had to be salted or smoked. Another important job was to care for the children. Mothers taught their daughters all those skills.

Children worked hard on the farm. Young boys and girls picked berries, carried water, and fed the chickens. They baby-sat the younger kids. Some older children wanted to be farmers. Some of them wanted to learn to be a craftsperson. A **craftsperson** is someone who makes things for other people. Children learned a **craft** by being an **apprentice** to a skilled worker.

There were all kinds of craftspeople in Plymouth. At first, people did not use money to buy the things the craftspeople made. They would barter. **Barter** means to trade one thing for another. For example, the farmer gave the miller the grains he needed. The miller turned the grains into flour for the farmer. The jobs of craftspeople were very important.

MATERIALS

- pages 67–69, reproduced for each student
- 9" x 12" (23 x 30.5 cm) colored construction paper
- crayons or marking pens
- scissors
- glue
- hole punch
- metal ring

JOBS IN PLYMOUTH COLONY

Students learn about the different jobs craftspeople had in colonial America. They choose their favorite job and "set up shop."

STEPS TO FOLLOW

1. Distribute pages 67 and 68 to students. Read and talk about the different jobs highlighted on the pages.

2. Have the students color and cut out the eight job cards. Punch holes in each card and attach them all together with a metal ring.

3. The students then choose one of the eight jobs to use for the next part of the activity. Tell students to pretend they own a shop in Plymouth. They should choose which job they think sounds the most interesting to have had.

4. On the colonial shop sign pattern on page 69, students design their own sign. Tell students to include the name of their shop, the proprietor's name, and what product(s) are made there.

5. Have students decorate and cut out the sign. They should glue the sign to construction paper and then cut around it to make a border.

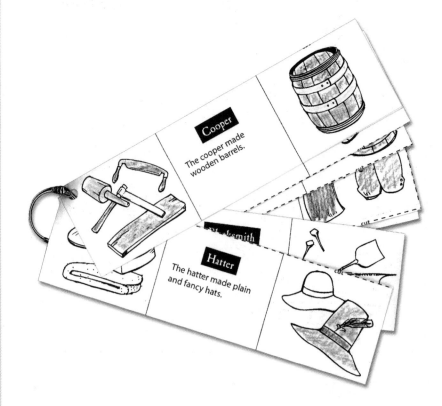

   EMC 3700 • Life in Plymouth Colony • ©2003 by Evan-Moor Corp.

JOB CARDS

Blacksmith
The blacksmith made things out of iron.

cut

Cobbler
The cobbler fixed the shoes and the boots.

cut

Cooper
The cooper made wooden barrels.

cut

Hatter
The hatter made plain and fancy hats.

JOB CARDS

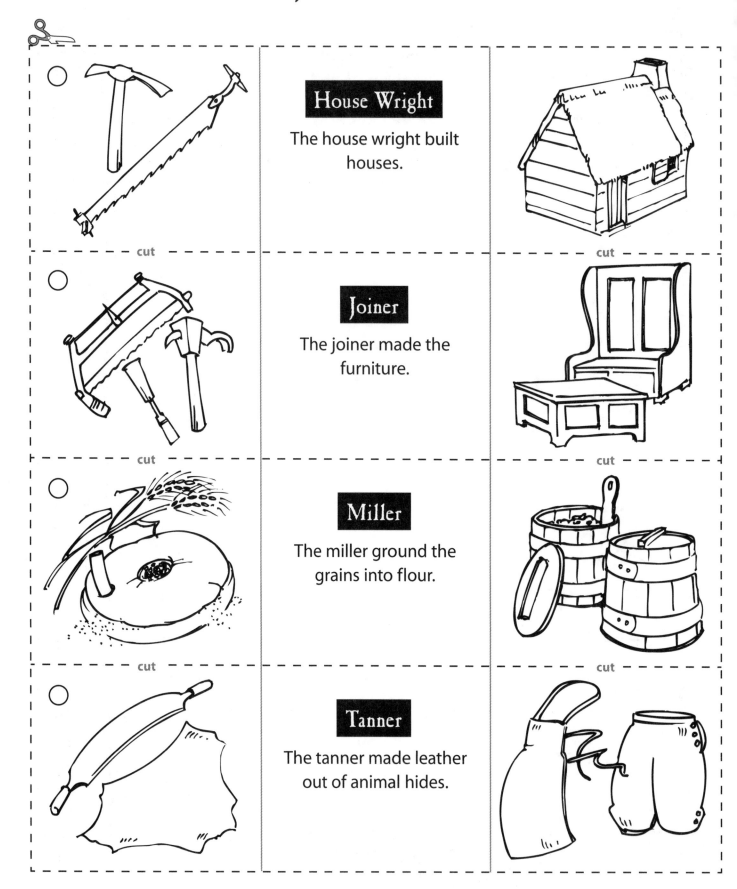

House Wright

The house wright built houses.

cut

Joiner

The joiner made the furniture.

cut

Miller

The miller ground the grains into flour.

cut

Tanner

The tanner made leather out of animal hides.

COLONIAL SHOP SIGN

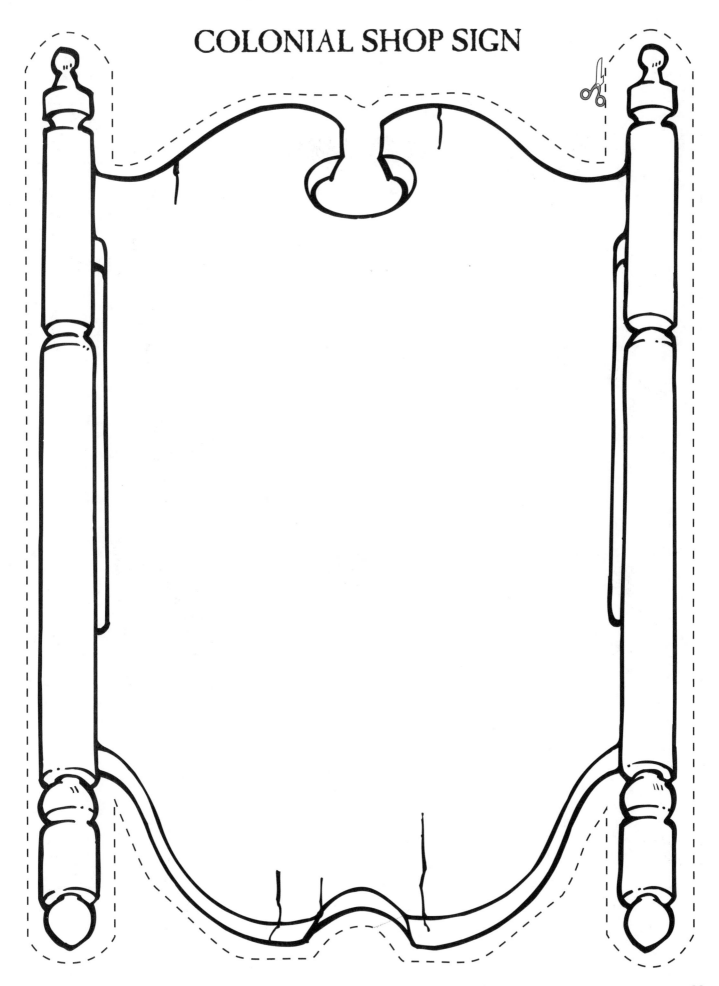

MY QUILTING BOOK

Women in colonial America created beautiful patchwork quilts. They often met for a quilting bee—a day of stitching and socializing. Students create a quilt book of their own.

STEPS TO FOLLOW

1. Read the information on quilts from page 71 together. Show real quilts if possible.

2. Distribute pages 72 and 73 to students and talk about the quilt designs.

3. Direct students to decorate each of the four squares using crayons, colored pencils, or marking pens. Encourage students to include designs such as polka dots and gingham checks, rather than just coloring in with solid colors.

4. Then have students design their own quilt square on page 71.

5. Instruct students to cut out all the quilt squares and the quilt information box. Glue each one onto a construction paper square.

6. Direct students to punch holes in the upper left-hand corner of each square.

7. Put the quilt squares in an order of your choosing. The information box may be used as the cover of the book.

8. Instruct students to thread the ribbon through all the holes and tie.

9. Encourage students to share their new quilting books with the class.

MATERIALS

- pages 71–73, reproduced for each student
- six 6" x 6" (15 x 15 cm) pieces of construction paper
- crayons, colored pencils, or marking pens
- scissors
- glue
- hole punch
- 12" (30.5 cm) ribbon

Colonial Quilts

Women in colonial America made beautiful patchwork quilts. They often met for a quilting bee. At a quilting bee, everyone worked on a quilt together and had a good time talking. Patchwork quilts were made from cloth pieces left over when new clothes were made. Sometimes pieces of fabric were cut from worn out clothes. Each small piece of cloth had to be stitched to a large backing piece. Quilting patterns had names that described the shapes.

EMC 3700 • Life in Plymouth Colony • ©2003 by Evan-Moor Corp.

QUILT PATTERNS

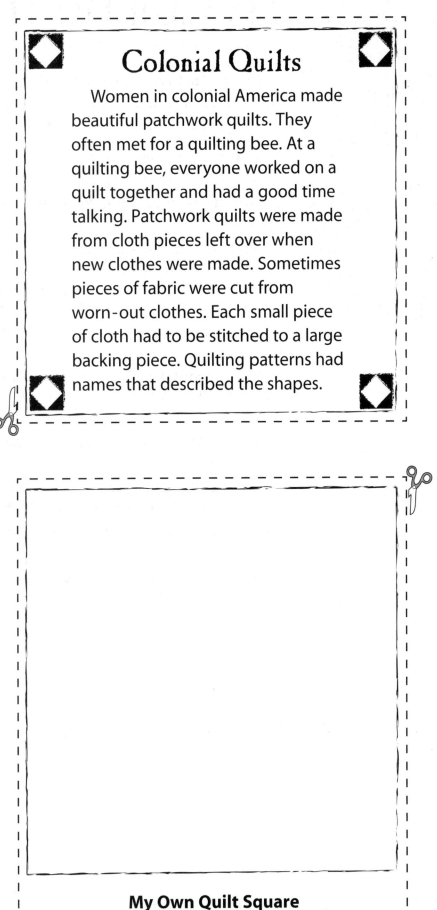

Colonial Quilts

Women in colonial America made beautiful patchwork quilts. They often met for a quilting bee. At a quilting bee, everyone worked on a quilt together and had a good time talking. Patchwork quilts were made from cloth pieces left over when new clothes were made. Sometimes pieces of fabric were cut from worn-out clothes. Each small piece of cloth had to be stitched to a large backing piece. Quilting patterns had names that described the shapes.

My Own Quilt Square

QUILT PATTERNS

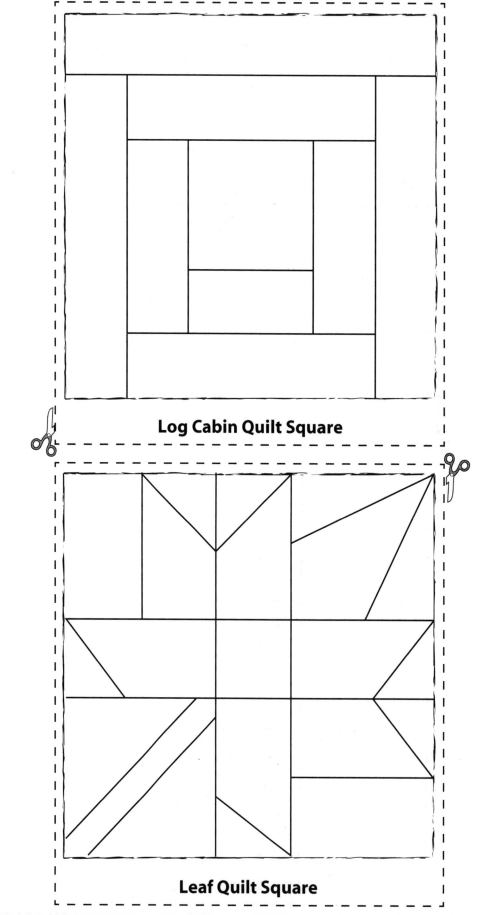

Log Cabin Quilt Square

Leaf Quilt Square

 EMC 3700 • Life in Plymouth Colony • ©2003 by Evan-Moor Corp.

QUILT PATTERNS

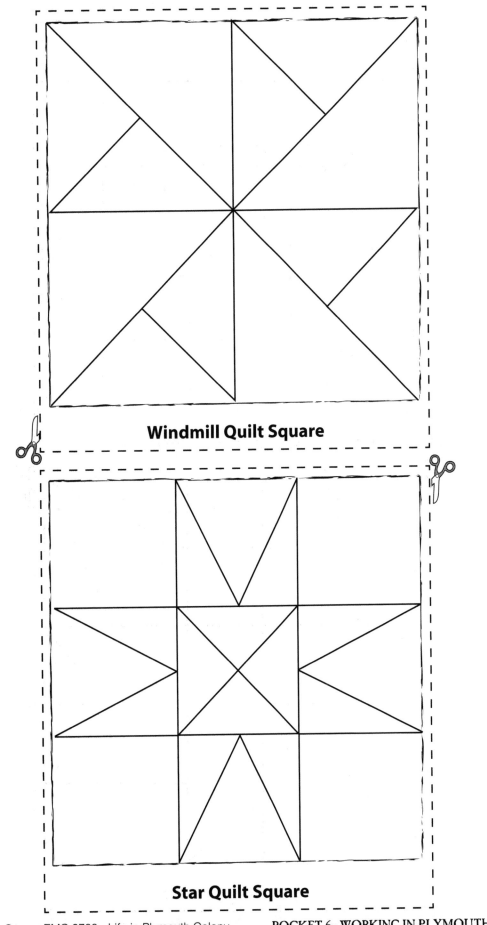

Windmill Quilt Square

Star Quilt Square

Pocket 7

GOING TO SCHOOL

CUT AND PASTE

See page 2 for information on how to prepare the pocket label. See page 16 for information on how to prepare the "Words to Know" activity.

FACT SHEET

Read the background information to familiarize yourself with schools in Plymouth Colony. Share the information with your students as appropriate. Incorporate library and multimedia resources that are available.

STUDENT BOOKLET

See page 2 for information on how to prepare the student booklet. Read and discuss the information booklet as a class. Encourage students to read their booklets to partners or independently.

ACTIVITIES

Students learn about a special kind of schoolbook called a hornbook. They make a hornbook and then use it to practice their writing.

The New England Primer was a colonial textbook that students used to learn their alphabet. Students make an accordion book using some of the rhyming couplets from the book to see how children learned their alphabet letters.

GOING TO
SCHOOL

©2003 by Evan-Moor Corp. • EMC 3700

penmanship

schoolmaster

dame school

hornbook

GOING TO SCHOOL

The Pilgrims felt that everyone should learn to read the Word of God (the Bible), so education was important to them. There were no formal schools in Plymouth during the early 1600s. At first, children were taught at home. Parents expected their children to read, write, and add. Mothers taught the children, or they had a neighbor help the children with their lessons.

The first schools were called dame schools. They were called dame schools because women taught the children in their kitchens. The younger children learned how to read, usually from the Bible. They were taught simple math because they were expected to know how to count and to add.

The children in the dame school used a special kind of schoolbook called a hornbook. A hornbook was a wooden paddle that had a piece of paper tacked to it. It had the letters of the alphabet, simple vowel and consonant combinations, and the Lord's Prayer written on it. A thin layer shaved off a cow's horn protected the paper. Children used a sharp stick and traced over the lessons on the hornbook. Once the children learned to read and write everything that was on the hornbook, they were finished with dame school.

After dame school, boys were allowed to go to another school to learn. Girls were supposed to stay home. Most Pilgrims thought it was more important for girls to learn domestic skills than to continue a formal education.

In 1647 the first law regarding schools was passed in the Massachusetts Bay Colony. The Plymouth Colony followed their lead later by requiring children to go to school. The laws stated that any town with 50 or more families had to have a grade school. The school was a one-room building. Students sat on hard benches in straight rows facing the teacher. Students were required to bring wood for the fireplace. Students who brought in the most wood got to sit closest to the fire. Students who forgot had to sit in the back. Different age groups all learned from the same teacher.

Most of the teachers in these schools were men called schoolmasters. Women who taught in a school had to quit teaching when they got married. Teachers were very strict and expected the boys to behave. The schoolmasters kept birch branches handy and used them to whip the boys if they misbehaved. If students did not do their lessons, they were called dunces. Boys had to sit on dunce stools and wear dunce caps. Whispering to friends was not allowed. Schoolmasters had boys bite down on little sticks called whispering sticks to keep them quiet.

During a typical day, the boys learned reading, 'riting, and 'rithmetic—the "three Rs." Some of them also learned geography and history. The students read from a book called *The New England Primer*. The book was first published in 1690. The book contained the letters of the alphabet illustrated by rhyming couplets and woodcuts. There were prayers and moral lessons from the Old Testament. There were also many questions and answers about God. Students were expected to know everything in the book before graduating.

Students spent a lot of time learning to write neatly. Good penmanship was more important than spelling correctly. They copied their lessons repeatedly, using quill pens dipped into inkwells. They also spent time memorizing and reciting their lessons.

Formal schooling ended for most boys when they were about 13 years old. At that time, they learned a trade, either from their fathers or through an apprenticeship. Sons of richer families went on to college. The first college in colonial America was Harvard University in Boston, Massachusetts. The Puritans founded the college in 1636.

The Pilgrims of Plymouth believed that education was important to help their children become good, productive citizens.

Note: Reproduce pages 77–79 for students to use with the "Going to School Booklet" activity, as described on page 74.

GOING TO SCHOOL

The Pilgrims believed children should be good students. Children were taught at home when they were young. Mothers taught their children after chores were done. Sometimes a neighbor helped the children with their lessons. The children learned the "three Rs" at home. The three Rs were reading, 'riting, and 'rithmetic. The Pilgrims did not spell very well, so this is how they spelled reading, writing, and arithmetic.

At seven years old, some children went to **dame schools. Dame** means "woman." Women taught the children in their kitchens. The schoolbook they used was called a hornbook. A **hornbook** was a wooden paddle that had a piece of paper tacked to it. It had letters of the alphabet on it. A thin layer shaved from a cow's horn protected the paper. It looked like waxed paper over the paper. Children used a sharp stick and traced over the letters.

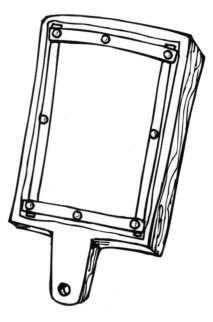

Some boys went to another school after they were finished with dame school. Girls stayed home. Pilgrims thought it was more important for girls to learn from their mothers than to go to school. The new school for the boys was in a one-room building. One teacher taught all the students from ages 7 to 13. Students sat on hard benches in straight rows.

   EMC 3700 • Life in Plymouth Colony • ©2003 by Evan-Moor Corp.

The teachers in these schools were mostly men called **schoolmasters.** Teachers were very strict. If a boy misbehaved, the teacher could hit him with a small tree branch. If students did not learn their lessons, the teachers might put dunce caps on their heads. That meant they were not smart. Boys could not even whisper in class. If they did, the teachers put little sticks in their mouths to keep them quiet.

The students read from a book called *The New England Primer.* The book had the alphabet, prayers, and lessons about how to be a good person. The students had to memorize and read aloud often. Students had to have good **penmanship.** They copied sentences using quill pens dipped in inkwells. At age 13, most boys quit school to go to work. Some richer boys went to a college like Harvard University in Boston before they got a job.

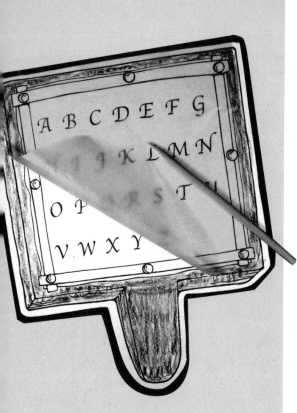

A HORNBOOK

Colonial children in dame school used a special kind of schoolbook called a hornbook. Students make this model of the hornbook and practice using it.

MATERIALS

- page 81, reproduced for each student
- 9" x 7" (23 x 18 cm) waxed paper
- 9" x 12" (23 x 30.5 cm) tagboard
- glue
- scissors
- piece of doweling (the diameter should be approximately the same as a standard pencil)
- stapler
- pencil sharpener

STEPS TO FOLLOW

1. Students cut out and glue the pattern to the tagboard. Then students trim the tagboard so that it is just larger than the pattern.

2. Students put the waxed paper on top of the pattern, covering the alphabet letters. The waxed paper is stapled in place at the top.

3. Students should trim the waxed paper to match the tagboard.

4. Insert the dowel in a pencil sharpener and sharpen until the end of the dowel is pointed, but not sharp.

5. Have students use the dowel to trace the alphabet letters on the waxed paper.

6. Discuss with students how the style of penmanship has changed from colonial times.

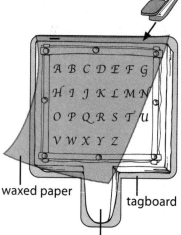

waxed paper   tagboard

hornbook pattern

A HORNBOOK

A B C D E F G

H I J K L M N

O P Q R S T U

V W X Y Z

Neat handwriting was very important to the colonists. Children copied their lessons repeatedly in their hornbooks. Some of the letters were formed differently than they are formed today.

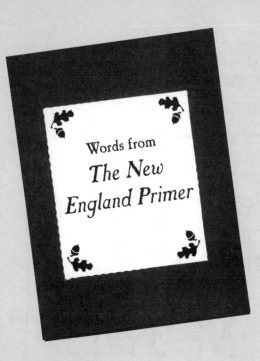

Words from *The New England Primer*

MATERIALS

- page 83, reproduced for each student
- 6" x 18" (15 x 45.5 cm) brown construction paper
- scissors
- glue

LEARNING TO READ

There were no storybooks and very few books with illustrations for children in Plymouth Colony. Students make this little book with words from *The New England Primer*.

STEPS TO FOLLOW

1. Students fold the brown paper as shown.

2. Students cut apart the book pages. The title piece is glued to the front.

3. Students glue the D through G alphabet squares on the inside pages. Glue the H alphabet square to the back.

4. Read the book with your students. Discuss how learning to read in Plymouth Colony was different from learning to read in your classroom.

Step 1

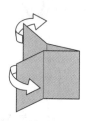

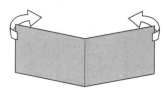

D — A Dog will bite A thief at night.

E — An Eagle's flight Is out of sight.

F — The idle Fool Is whipt at school.

G — As runs the Glass Man's life doth pass.

EMC 3700 • Life in Plymouth Colony • ©2003 by Evan-Moor Corp.

LEARNING TO READ

Words from *The New England Primer*

D

A Dog will bite
A thief at night.

E

An Eagle's flight
Is out of sight.

F

The idle Fool
Is whipt at school.

G

As runs the Glass
Man's life doth pass.

H

My book and Heart
Shall never part.

Pocket 8

WHAT DID THE PILGRIMS GIVE US?

CUT AND PASTE

Pocket Label, Words to Know .... **page 85**
See page 2 for information on how to prepare the pocket label. See page 16 for information on how to prepare the "Words to Know" activity.

FACT SHEET

What Did the Pilgrims Give Us?.......... **page 86**
Read the background information to familiarize yourself with what customs the Pilgrims gave us. Share the information with your students as appropriate. Incorporate library and multimedia resources that are available.

STUDENT BOOKLET

"What Did the Pilgrims Give Us?" Booklet.................. **pages 87–89**
See page 2 for information on how to prepare the student booklet. Read and discuss the information booklet as a class. Encourage students to read their booklets to partners or independently.

ACTIVITIES

Geese in the Garden .... **pages 90 & 91**
Pilgrim children did get to play a little. Children today still play with some of the same kinds of toys and games colonial children did. Students make a colonial toy of their own.

Hasty Pudding .... **pages 92 & 93**
Favorite recipes have been passed down from one generation to another. Mothers have been making hasty pudding since the 1600s. Students get to taste this colonial treat when they make it for the class.

Thank You, Pilgrims..................... **page 94**
Students write an acrostic poem to thank the Pilgrims for all the familiar customs and traditions they gave to America.

EMC 3700 • Life in Plymouth Colony • ©2003 by Evan-Moor Corp.

WHAT DID THE PILGRIMS GIVE US?

©2003 by Evan-Moor Corp. • EMC 3700

marketplace

herbs

manners

custom

FACT SHEET
WHAT DID THE PILGRIMS GIVE US?

The Pilgrims developed many traditional customs that are still used today in America. Both English and Native American customs from the New England area have made lasting impressions on the makeup of American society.

The Pilgrims helped to establish the hard-work ethic that is associated with America. The Pilgrims worked long days farming and in the trades. Farming was considered a noble profession and is still respected today. The Pilgrims brought with them from England a craft tradition and skills that helped establish different kinds of occupations in America. The custom of having master craftspeople share their talents with apprentices became common.

The Pilgrims came to America for religious freedom. The religious customs of the Pilgrims can be seen today. Some groups of people still see the Sabbath as a day of the week reserved for church services, rest, and religious contemplation. The "Sunday dinner" tradition was and is common in many homes. The Pilgrims had a special dinner between religious services on Sundays. The meal was prepared the day before because Sunday was considered a day of rest.

Good health was always a concern for the Pilgrims. They were plagued with deadly illnesses, including influenza, tuberculosis, smallpox, and pneumonia. Vitamin deficiencies were also common because very few people ate fresh fruits and vegetables. Because there were so few doctors, the Pilgrims had to rely on herbal remedies. It was the custom for women to grow herbs in their gardens. They had learned what herbs and wild plants were good from the local Native Americans. Plants like garlic, mustard, mint, and lavender were used to mix up home remedies. Medicinal herbs were ground and then boiled to be drunk or inhaled. Some were turned into a paste or ointment to put on the skin. The Pilgrims and the Native Americans knew that natural plants could help. Some of those same herbal treatments are used today.

Education was respected in colonial America, especially in New England. The Puritans believed the written word was important. When the Pilgrims became part of the Massachusetts Bay Colony, they could take advantage of better schools. They could even send their children to the first college, Harvard University, in Boston, Massachusetts. Books like the Bible, *The New England Primer,* and *The School of Manners* became standards for home and school.

The custom of having good manners was considered very important to the Pilgrims. Pilgrim parents taught their children proper behavior and manners using *The School of Manners* as a guide. One of the rules was that children had to stand to speak. Another one was that they were not supposed to run into the street. Children were not to insult their elders, but only show love and respect. There were also rules for eating. Children were not to spit, cough, or blow their noses at the table. They were not to stuff their mouths with too much food. The list goes on. Good manners are still considered virtues.

Even though the Pilgrims worked hard, they still had time for a little fun. Children could play after their chores were finished. They loved to play with hoops and sticks, balls, and marbles. Familiar games such as Leapfrog, Hopscotch, and Cat's Cradle started in colonial times. Those same kinds of games can be seen today on playgrounds across America.

Many other daily activities that Pilgrims enjoyed became customs. Women got together to make quilts in a gathering called a quilting bee. Farmers and craftspeople met in the village and set up booths to sell their livestock and their wares. They sold such things as quilts, candles, weather vanes, and fine furniture. Farmers' markets and county fairs are still common today.

Customs and traditions are important to any society. We can thank the Pilgrims for giving so many to America.

Note: Reproduce pages 87–89 for students to use with the "What Did the Pilgrims Give Us? Booklet" activity, as described on page 84.

WHAT DID THE PILGRIMS GIVE US?

The Pilgrims gave us many customs that we use today. A **custom** is something you do regularly for a long time. Another word for **custom** is "tradition." The Pilgrims thought being polite was important, so rules about good manners became a custom. The Pilgrim children played many games that are still played today. The Pilgrims celebrated the first Thanksgiving. That holiday has become a tradition in America.

The Pilgrims believed that children should have good **manners.** Parents used a book called *The School of Manners.* One rule in the book said that children should stand up to speak. Another rule was that children should not run or throw things into the street. Children were not supposed to stuff too much food into their mouths. Children could not spit, cough, or blow their noses at the table. Some of those rules for good manners became customs that are still followed today.

Pilgrims had to work hard, but they played, too. One game they played was called Leapfrog. The first player squatted down. The second player put his hands on the first player and then leaped over. Another game was called Hopscotch. Players jumped on squares they made in the dirt. These games are still played today. They have become customs.

Mothers had to be the doctors in Plymouth. They grew **herbs** in the garden to make medicine for the family. Women planted lavender, garlic, mustard, mint, and other plants. The women ground the plants, roots, and seeds into powder.

Then they boiled the powder in water to make a liquid medicine. Medicines always tasted bad, but they did help people get better. The custom of making medicines from plants is used today.

Many activities that the Pilgrims enjoyed became customs. The women made quilts together. They called this a quilting bee. Farmers and craftspeople set up booths at the **marketplace** in the village. People sold things like quilts, weather vanes, furniture, and homemade food. People still sell their homemade items at farmers' markets and county fairs. The Pilgrims gave Americans lots of customs like these.

MATERIALS

- page 91, reproduced for each student
- two 1¼" x 12" (3 x 30.5 cm) strips of tagboard
- 8½" x 11" (21.5 x 28 cm) tagboard or file folder
- glue
- marking pens
- 4 paper fasteners
- hole punch
- scissors

GEESE IN THE GARDEN

Children in Plymouth Colony had many chores to do, but on Sunday after services, no one was allowed to work. The entire family rested and spent the day together. This model is a "Sunday toy." Adults and children would play with it together. The real toy would have been made of wood.

STEPS TO FOLLOW

1. Have students color and cut out the two geese and the garden from page 91.

2. Direct them to glue the cutouts to tagboard and cut around the pieces to make the cutouts sturdier. Punch holes in the geese as shown.

Step 2

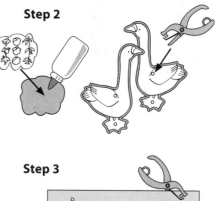

3. Punch holes in both tagboard strips about 2" (5 cm) from each end.

Step 3

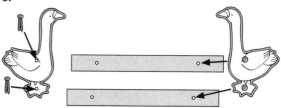

4. Fasten the geese to the tagboard strips using paper fasteners.

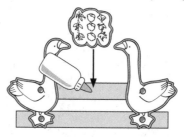

5. Glue the garden to the middle of the top strip.

6. Hold the bottom strip. Push and pull the top strip to see the geese peck at the vegetables.

GEESE IN THE GARDEN

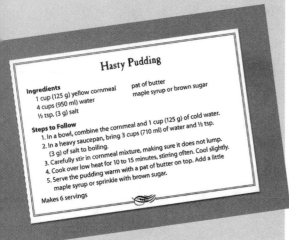

Hasty Pudding

Ingredients
1 cup (125 g) yellow cornmeal
4 cups (950 ml) water
½ tsp. (3 g) salt

pat of butter
maple syrup or brown sugar

Steps to Follow
1. In a bowl, combine the cornmeal and 1 cup (125 g) of cold water.
2. In a heavy saucepan, bring 3 cups (710 ml) of water and ½ tsp. (3 g) of salt to boiling.
3. Carefully stir in cornmeal mixture, making sure it does not lump.
4. Cook over low heat for 10 to 15 minutes, stirring often. Cool slightly.
5. Serve the pudding warm with a pat of butter on top. Add a little maple syrup or sprinkle with brown sugar.

Makes 6 servings

MATERIALS

- page 93, reproduced for two students
- 6" x 9" (15 x 23 cm) construction paper
- pencil
- scissors
- glue
- ingredients and supplies for recipe on page 93
- small bowls or one large bowl
- spoons

HASTY PUDDING

Women made a variety of recipes using cornmeal. Hasty pudding was a popular wintertime treat for the Pilgrims.

Using a colonial recipe, students follow the steps to make hasty pudding.

STEPS TO FOLLOW

1. Talk about the custom of passing down favorite recipes to family and friends. Tell students that the recipe for hasty pudding has been around since the 1600s.

2. Read and discuss the recipe on page 93. Use this recipe to make a simple treat for the class. This may be done as a demonstration, or you may want the students to work in small groups to make the pudding.

3. To be authentic, you may want to have students use spoons and sample the pudding right out of the pot, just as colonial children did.

4. Direct students to cut out the recipe card and glue it to construction paper, cutting around the edge.

Hasty Pudding

Ingredients

1 cup (125 g) yellow cornmeal

4 cups (950 ml) water

½ tsp. (3 g) salt

pat of butter

maple syrup or brown sugar

Steps to Follow

1. In a bowl, combine the cornmeal and 1 cup (240 ml) of cold water.
2. In a heavy saucepan, bring 3 cups (710 ml) of water and ½ tsp. (3 g) of salt to boiling.
3. Carefully stir in cornmeal mixture, making sure it does not lump.
4. Cook over low heat for 10 to 15 minutes, stirring often. Cool slightly.
5. Serve the pudding warm with a pat of butter on top. Add a little maple syrup or sprinkle with brown sugar.

Makes 6 servings

Hasty Pudding

Ingredients

1 cup (125 g) yellow cornmeal

4 cups (950 ml) water

½ tsp. (3 g) salt

pat of butter

maple syrup or brown sugar

Steps to Follow

1. In a bowl, combine the cornmeal and 1 cup (240 ml) of cold water.
2. In a heavy saucepan, bring 3 cups (710 ml) of water and ½ tsp. (3 g) of salt to boiling.
3. Carefully stir in cornmeal mixture, making sure it does not lump.
4. Cook over low heat for 10 to 15 minutes, stirring often. Cool slightly.
5. Serve the pudding warm with a pat of butter on top. Add a little maple syrup or sprinkle with brown sugar.

Makes 6 servings

MATERIALS

- 6" x 18" (15 x 45.5 cm) white construction paper
- pencil
- crayons or marking pens

THANK YOU, PILGRIMS

Students get a chance to think about all the things that the Pilgrims gave America when they write an acrostic poem.

STEPS TO FOLLOW

1. As a class, review the customs and traditions the Pilgrims gave to America, using the fact sheet and student booklet as references.

2. Direct students to accordion-fold the construction paper into eight 2¼" (6 cm) sections.

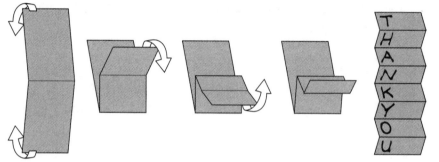

3. Students turn the paper so it is vertical, and then write the letters spelling "thank you," one letter per section.

4. Instruct students to write or draw something the Pilgrims gave us that corresponds with the letter in each of the eight sections. Encourage students to look back through their pockets and their Words to Know dictionary for help. For example, *T* may stand for *turkey, tanning leather,* or *town crier.*

Note: You may choose to do Step 4 as a class activity, and then have the students copy the class ideas from the chalkboard onto their accordion books.

A LETTER FROM LONG AGO

Directions: Pretend you are a Pilgrim boy or girl and write a letter to a friend back in England. Tell your friend about all the things you have to do in one day.

_____

date

Dear _____,

My family built a new house in Plymouth. We like it here. There is a lot of work to do every day.

In the morning, I _____

_____

_____

_____.

In the afternoon, I _____

_____

_____

_____

_____.

In the evening, I _____

_____

_____

_____.

I miss you. I hope you can move to Plymouth, too.

Your friend,

_____

REMEMBERING THE PILGRIMS

Directions: Look at the book of pockets you have made about Life in Plymouth Colony. Finish each sentence with your favorite memory from the pockets.

1. The name of my favorite booklet that I made was

   _____.

2. My four favorite words I learned from the Words to Know flap book are

   _____   _____

   _____   _____

3. This is what I remember most about the voyage of the Pilgrims:

   _____.

4. This is what I remember most about the Pilgrims landing in the New World:

   _____.

5. This is what I remember most about the Pilgrim village:

   _____.

6. This is what I remember most about a Pilgrim home:

   _____.

7. This is what I remember most about working in Plymouth:

   _____.

8. This is what I remember most about schools in Plymouth:

   _____.

   EMC 3700 • Life in Plymouth Colony • ©2003 by Evan-Moor Corp.